JAMES HEPBURN

BORN, 1747   DIED, 1817

GENEALOGY AND HISTORY OF
THE HEPBURN FAMILY
OF THE SUSQUEHANNA VALLEY

WITH
REFERENCE TO OTHER
FAMILIES OF THE SAME NAME

Remember the days of old,
Consider the years of many generations:
Ask thy father and he will shew thee;
Thy elders, and they will Tell thee.
—Deuteronomy, xxxii, 7.

John F. Meginnes

Author of Otzinachson, Biography of
Frances Slocum, Historical Journal, etc.

HERITAGE BOOKS
2012

HERITAGE BOOKS

AN IMPRINT OF HERITAGE BOOKS, INC.

Books, CDs, and more—Worldwide

For our listing of thousands of titles see our website
at
www.HeritageBooks.com

A Facsimile Reprint
Published 2012 by
HERITAGE BOOKS, INC.
Publishing Division
100 Railroad Ave. #104
Westminster, Maryland 21157

Originally published
Williamsport, P.A.
Gazette & Bulletin Printing House
1894

International Standard Book Numbers
Paperbound: 978-0-7884-1789-4
Clothbound: 978-0-7884-9271-6

TO THE READER.

That the desire for a knowledge of family genealogy is growing rapidly, and taking deep root in the minds of the people, is no longer doubtful. To know something of one's ancestry is a thought uppermost in the minds of thousands. This is attested by the many family histories that have been written in recent years, and the many that are still in course of preparation. Annual family reunions and meetings for the purpose of conferring together and collecting and preserving family records are another evidence of this growing sentiment, and as the years roll on they are likely to increase.

The preparation and publication of this book came about in this way : Sometime in 1882 I met my personal friend, Hon. L. A. Mackey, in Lock Haven, and he made an earnest request that I should undertake the task of writing the " History of the Hepburn Family of the Susquehanna Valley." On replying that I felt incompetent to undertake such a work, Mr. Mackey quickly replied: " *The time has come; you must do it!*" We soon after parted and little more was thought of the matter until the sudden death of my friend in February, 1889, recalled his request made seven years before. Still the beginning of the work was deferred from time to time, mainly on account of the difficulty involved in such an undertaking.

About the close of 1891 Mr. Robert Hopewell Hepburn, of Avondale, made a similar request and insisted that I should undertake the work, at the same time proffering his aid and assistance in the undertaking. Seeing that there was no way of escape, except by a flat refusal, the work of gathering the materials and consulting authorities was commenced and pursued until in the autumn of 1894 it was finished, so far as the original scope had been outlined.

The earnest request of my deceased, as well as living, friend has now been complied with, so far as I have been able, and the result is herewith presented. That it will be found imperfect in some respects there is little doubt; that errors will be detected is probable, for in sifting and condensing the mass of materials which had been collected largely by correspondence, transcribing the names and dates of births, marriages and deaths of many persons, it would be passing strange if no errors were committed. No perfect book has yet been written, and never will be until man is perfect. Those who discover errors, therefore, will please cover them with the mantle of charity.

The history of this family is one which possesses absorbing interest from the earliest times to the present. Few families in the course of four or five centuries can show a continuous line of more distinguished members—of members who have been eminent in the professions of law, theology and medicine; of members who have distinguished themselves as orators, scholars, soldiers, statesmen and politicians. Descendants of this long and illustrious line have reason not only to feel proud of their Scottish ancestors, but to honor and revere their names and memories.

To those who aided in furnishing information, and by their influence encouraged the work, my acknowledgments are due and warmly tendered, and especially to Mr. R. H. Hepburn, of Avondale, and Mrs. Anna H. Watts, of Carlisle, Pa. My humble work is done.

JOHN F. MEGINNESS.

Williamsport, Pa., December 1, 1894.

THE HEPBURN FAMILY.

JAMES AND WILLIAM HEPBURN were prominent and representative men in the West Branch Valley of the Susquehanna one hundred years ago. The latter came as early as 1773, from Ireland, and at once became identified with the struggling pioneer settlers in their efforts to repel the savages. The former, who spent about ten years in and about Philadelphia, did not locate here until about the close of the Revolutionary war, when he engaged in the mercantile business, and the buying and selling of land. Through sagacity, business tact and enterprise, he accumulated a handsome competence; William became a State Senator, and it was largely through his efforts that Lycoming County was organized April 13, 1795, and as a recognition of his services he was appointed the first judge. And working together, the two brothers were prime movers in laying the foundation of what is now the beautiful and flourishing city of Williamsport, Pa.

ORIGIN OF THE FAMILY NAME.

The Hepburn family was of Scotch origin and of high antiquity, the house having been founded as early as 1200. It is not positively known how the name came into existence, but there is a tradition that it originated from the names of two rivers. In early times, before Christian names were adopted, families were often designated by a title corresponding with some object in the neighborhood where they lived. This surname underwent many changes in the course of the ages. It is probable, therefore, that the family originally lived near two streams from which the name Heborn was deduced. In course of time it was changed to Hebron, then Hepborn, and finally the transition to Hepburn was easy. In France, where members of the family were held in high esteem during the fifteenth, sixteenth and seventeenth centuries, the name was written d'Hebron, d'Hepburne, and sometimes Esbron. During the last two hundred years the name in Scotland and America has almost universally been written Hepburn, although there are a few in this country who still write it Hepborn.

Before proceeding with the history of James and William, and their descendants, let us look into the history of the early families,—for there were several,—that we may better understand their distinguished ancestry. It will not be attempted, however, in these preliminary remarks, to follow anything like a connected line of descent in Scotland, because at this late day that would be almost impossible, inasmuch as the origin of the family dates back fully seven hundred years. Investigations of the early history have been mostly confined to Burton, who is pretty generally conceded to be the fullest and most accurate of Scottish historians, for the purpose merely of showing some of the leading and representative members of the different houses and the stirring and exciting events with which they were connected.

Many members of the family in early times occupied prominent positions in civil and military life, were distinguished as ecclesiastics, poets, divines, judges and advocates, and were more or less identified with the fierce political and religious dissensions which so disturbed Scotland during the sixteenth and seventeenth centuries. Others sat in Parliament and assisted in the framing of laws, whilst others were entrusted with their administration. One married a Scottish queen, another distinguished himself as a soldier in the service of Gustavus Adolphus and Louis XIIIth., and became a Marshal of France, whilst another was prominent in the great battle of Waterloo.

In 1488, in the early part of the reign of James III., when

there was much political friction, as well as many conspiracies, to obtain the mastery, Burton says (Vol. III., p. 32,):
"Doubtless in the confederacy there were several leaders
stimulated by personal wrong or disappointment. For instance, the Howes and Hepburns on the border were angry
that the revenues of the Priory of Coldingham, which they
sought to divide between them, should be devoted to the
support of the King's favorite choir in the Chapel Royal of
Sterling. But the confederacy, though it might have been
helped from such quarrels, rested on broken ground."

EARLS OF BOTHWELL.

In the peerage of Scotland the Earls of Bothwell, who
were members of the Hepburn family, occupy a conspicuous position in history. The rank or title was not fully
created before 1488. During a disturbance, when James
III. was on the throne, a rebellious party, headed by Douglas,
seized a number of his adherents at the Bridge of Lauder
and hanged them before the King's eyes. A young man
named Ramsay was saved, and James IV., who had raised
the standard of rebellion (see Encyclopedia Brittannica, p.
3593,) against his father, created him titular Earl of Bothwell. Ramsay very much desired the title in full, but the
Hepburns had a firm grip on it. "They were of an ancient
race, these Hepburns of Hailes," says Burton, and were
able to control the appointment. James III. was assassin-
ated in 1488, and his son, James IV., succeeded him, when
the question of the earlship was decided.

I. Patrick Hepburn, third Lord Hailes, was made the
first Earl of Bothwell. He was the eldest son of Adam,
second Lord Hailes, and Helen, eldest daughter of Alexander, first Lord Howe. He was Governor of the Castle
of Berwick and defended it for a time in 1482, when the
town was invested by the English, but afterwards surren-
dered. After a long and eventful history he died at Edin-

burgh, October 17, 1508.   By his wife, Lady Janet Douglas, only daughter of James, first Earl of Morton, he had three sons and three daughters, viz.: 1. Adam, second Earl of Bothwell. 2. John, Bishop of Brechin. 3. Patrick, Bishop of Moray.   4. Janet, married George, fourth Lord Seton. 5. Mary, married Archibard, Earl of Angus. 6. Margaret, married Henry, Lord Sinclair.

The grandfather of the first Earl, Patrick of Hailes, was the warm friend of Jane Beaufort, widow of James I., who died in 1436.   She spent her last days under his hospitable roof in the Castle of Dunbar.

With the first Earl of Bothwell we have the beginning of a long and distinguished line of descent which has spread widely over two continents.   And at this point the reader is particularly enjoined to note the name of Janet which appears at this stage of the history, as it may serve as an important connecting link in the line of female descent before the close.

II.   Adam, the second Earl of Bothwell, first son of the first Earl, fell by the side of his king, James IV., in the battle of Flodden Field, September 9, 1513.

III.   Patrick Hepburn, third Earl of Bothwell (1512–1556), was the only son of Adam, second Earl of Bothwell, by his wife Agnes Stewart, married in 1511, natural daughter of James, Earl of Buchan, and full brother of James II. He was still a minor when his father fell on the field of Flodden, September 9, 1513.   The young earl, along with the Master of Hailes and other Hepburns, received remission for treasonable assistance of Lord Howe.   Patrick was known as the "Fair Earl."   He married Agnes Sinclair. She belonged to a Norman family, and became the mother of a daughter, Jane or Janet, and a son, James, who was destined to figure more conspicuously in Scottish history than any one member of the Hepburn family.   The history of

Patrick is long and eventful. In 1543 he divorced his wife and died September, 1556, at Dumfries. The mother was always warmly attached to her son James, and was in fact his good angel. She died in 1573.

IV. James Hepburn, fourth Earl of Bothwell, only son of Patrick, third Earl, by his wife Agnes, daughter of Lord Henry Sinclair, was born probably in 1526. He was brought up for the most part in the palace—Spynie Castle—of his relative, Patrick Hepburn, Bishop of Moray. He was well educated under the Bishop. Having been born the most richly endowed and powerful nobleman in Scotland but one, great honors sought him early in life. Notwithstanding the divorce of his father and mother in 1543, James on the death of his father in September, 1556, obtained unquestioned possession of the titles and estates, as well as the hereditary offices of Lord High Admiral of Scotland, Sheriff of Berwick, Haddington and Edinburgh, and also baillie of Lauderdale, with the custody of Hailes and Crichton. Before he was of age he sat in Parliament, and when but twenty-eight he was a lieutenant-general. His father died reconciled to the queen dowager. Some time towards the close of 1560 (see Encyclopedia Brittannica) he appears to have been one of the lords who went over to France to meet the new Scottish Queen, Mary. In 1562 occurred the singular and obscure episode of the conspiracy between Bothwell and Arran to carry off the Queen. Arran was well known to be deeply enamored of Mary, and Bothwell intended to use this passion as a means of furthering his own designs against Murray. The plot, or the germ of it, was discovered; Arran was found to be almost insane, and an indictment was laid against Bothwell, who fled to France and remained there till 1565, when he returned. Bothwell (James Hepburn) was married February 24, 1566, to Lady Jane Gordon. He is described by the early writers as a singularly handsome man, of ma-

jestic mien and captivating manners. The times in which
he lived were rife with political plots and conspiracies to obtain power. Being a very ambitious man, it is not strange,
perhaps, to find him taking such an active part in many of
the schemes of the period. Morals, too, were at a very low
ebb, and there was little hesitancy on the part of political
aspirants to resort to extreme violence to remove opponents.

When James Hepburn (Bothwell) returned from France
the part he had borne in the plot against the Queen had not
been forgotten by the leaders, who feared him, because he
stood in their way of political advancement. The charge
against him was renewed by the Earl of Murray (or Moray),
one of the most desperate and unscrupulous conspirators of
the time, and the day of trial fixed. But as Murray's
forces and retainers were too numerous for Hepburn to
make his appearance with safety, he again fled. He re-
appeared at court in a short time after the marriage of
Queen Mary with her cousin, young Darnley, and began to
rise rapidly in royal favor. After the murder of Rizzio, the
Queen's Italian secretary, by a band of conspirators, Hepburn escaped from the palace and with great promptitude
drew together some armed forces for the Queen's protection. This movement elevated him greatly in royal esteem,
and from this time onward he was in the highest favor with
Mary and all-powerful at court. Some time in 1566 he was
dangerously wounded when on a judicial tour in Lidder-
dale. And while suffering from his wound, the Queen paid
him a visit, riding all the way from Jedburg, where she had
been attending to some official business. The fatigue of
this ride of forty miles brought on a severe illness which
came near terminating her life. After recovery the project
of a divorce from Darnley was mooted, but she declined to
favor it. This resulted in his assassination by blowing up
the building in which he was sleeping. Public opinion was
greatly inflamed over the affair, and charges were made

that Bothwell was concerned in the conspiracy, although it never was clearly established that he had a hand in it. He was too powerful to be dealt with by the law, and his enemies, of whom he had many of the most violent kind, were forced to remain passive.

On the 24th of April Bothwell played his last card by carrying off Queen Mary to Dunbar Castle, which she had granted him some time before. A divorce from his wife (Lady Jane Gordon) had been procured May 3, 1567, and on the 15th of the same month the royal marriage with Mary was completed. She had a few days previously pardoned Bothwell for his abduction of her, and had raised him to the rank of Duke of Orkney, which showed that she was not unwilling to speedily enter into new marriage relations, if indeed she was not a strong party to the scheme to hurry it along.

This marriage caused a great sensation in Scotland, as well as England, and the aspirants for political places at once took advantage of the excited state of public feeling to turn the people against Mary and her new husband. The great lords, enemies of Bothwell, collected their forces and seizing Edinburgh, precipitated a political revolution. Bothwell and the Queen escaped with the greatest difficulty to Dunbar. At Carberry Hill the opposing parties met, and after some parleying, Mary abdicated in favor of her infant son, with Moray as Regent.

Bothwell then parted from Mary forever and fled to Dunbar. This exciting event in Scottish history took place June 15, 1567, less than a month after their marriage. Finding that it was unsafe to remain in the kingdom, Bothwell sailed for Spynie Castle, north of Elgin, the residence of his aged great uncle, Patrick Hepburn, Bishop of Moray, by whom he had been brought up. Still being closely pursued, he took ship, but was captured by a Danish cruiser and carried to Copenhagen. The Danish authorities refusing to give him up, he was removed to Malmo, and afterwards to Draxholm Castle, where he died April 19, 1578, after having been in exile about ten years.

Mary fled to England and claimed the protection of Queen Elizabeth, but her sad fate, February 8, 1586, is well known to the general reader.

James Hepburn, Earl of Bothwell, was married three times. His first wife was a Dane, the second Lady Jane Gordon, and the third Mary Queen of Scots. His career was a stormy and exciting one. Owing to the bitterness existing between the rival factions in the times in which he lived, every opportunity was taken to misrepresent his motives and malign his character. General DePeyster, in his historical and analytical work on Bothwell, arrives at the conclusion that he was more sinned against than sinning. And this seems to be the consensus of opinion of nearly all modern writers on the subject. He always entertained an intense hatred of England, which undoubtedly had something to do with moulding the feeling of opposition to him, which was expressed by the writers of that time, and prevented them from doing him full justice. His natural ability and intellectual attainments were so much superior to the majority of the political aspirants of the times, that his successes created envy, and desperate efforts were made to ruin him. We have had plenty of examples of this kind in the history of our own country, when envious, vicious and narrow-minded politicians have stooped to injure and even destroy their successful rivals.

By his flight from Scotland James Hepburn sacrificed his magnificent estates and costly gifts from the crown. For the times in which he lived, and the emoluments he enjoyed, he was reputed a very wealthy man. But consuming ambition, the allurements of royalty, and the weakness for power, caused everything to vanish like the mists of the morning before the rays of the sun, and he died in poverty and exile.

V. Francis Stewart-Hepburn, fifth Earl of Bothwell, was the eldest son of John Stewart, Prior of Coldingham, and brother of the Regent Moray. His mother was Lady Jane Hepburn, only daughter of the third Earl, and sister of James, the fourth Earl. On the 29th of July, 1576, it being wrongfully supposed that his uncle had died in Denmark, he was created the fifth Earl of Bothwell, and appointed to many of his uncle's offices. His political career was stormy, and at one time he was compelled to fly to France. In time he returned and was engaged in military operations, but fortune going against him, he took refuge in Italy and died at Naples in 1624. He had three sons and three daughters, viz.: 1. Francis. 2. John, who became Prior of Coldingham, and got the houses and baronies belonging to that Priory united in a barony in 1621. 3. Henry, who also obtained a part of the lordship of Coldingham in 1621. 4. Elizabeth, who married James, second son of William, first Lord Cranston. 5. Margaret, married Alan, fifth Lord Cathcart. 6. Helen, married Macfarlane of Macfarlane.

BISHOP OF MORAY.

Patrick Hepburn, Bishop of Moray, was the natural son of Patrick, first Earl of Bothwell. Scotch history informs us that the Bishop was educated under his relative, John Hepburn, Prior of St. Andrews, whom he succeeded in the Priory in 1522. From 1524 to 1527 he held the office of Secretary to James V. of Scotland. He was prosecuted as accessory to the murder of Darnley, but acquitted November 28, 1567. He died at Spynie Castle June 20, 1573. He had seven sons and two daughters, but unfortunately their names are unknown to the writer.

John Hepburn, Prior of St. Andrews, and founder of St.

Leonard's College, was the fourth son of Adam Hepburn, second Lord Hailes, by Helen, eldest daughter of Alexander, first Lord Howe. He studied in Paris and wrote an elegant poem on hunting. He succeeded William Carron as Prior of the Convent in 1482. January 14, 1488, he obtained from the King the custody of the Castle of Falkland for five years. He was for some time keeper of the privy seal, and is mentioned, May 31, 1504, as Vicar General of St. Andrews. In 1512 he founded the College of St. Leonard, which he endowed. In 1514 he was a competitor with Gavin Douglas for the Archbishopric of St. Andrews, but failed. It was arranged that his brother, James Hepburn, should be made Bishop of Moray. Towards the close of his life he surrounded the Priory of St. Leonard's College with a wall, a considerable portion of which—known as the Abbey wall—is said to be still standing, and at various parts bears his arms and initials with the motto, *Ad Vitam*. He died in 1522. His monument still stands in St. Leonard's Chapel, but so worn by the elements as to be unreadable.

James Hepburn, born in 1573, in the shire of East Lothian, was the fourth son of Thomas Hepburn, rector of Oldhamstocks. He was a Catholic and a great scholar, and succeeded in mastering nearly all the languages of Europe. He lived at Rome for five years. During his life he did a prodigious amount of literary work, being the author of twenty-nine books and pamphlets. He died at Venice in 1620.

GALLANT SOLDIERS OF FORTUNE.

Sir John Hepburn, a soldier of fortune, was one of the most remarkable men of his time. His history may be found in full in a work entitled "Memoirs and Adventures of Sir John Hepburn," by James Grant, a Scottish writer of reputation. From this work it is learned that he was

descended from a long line of illustrious ancestors, the Hep-
burns of Hailes and Bothwell (who deduced their blood
from Sir Adam Hepburn, a distinguished warrior under
Robert Bruce, from whom he obtained the lands of North
Hailes and Traprene.) He was the second son of George
Hepburn of Athelstaneford, a small property in East
Lothian, which was held feudally of their kinsmen, the
Hepburns of Waughton.

Grant says that the earliest notice of the family occurs
on the 24th of November, 1569, when George of Athelstaneford was cited before an assize for killing a certain party
and wounding others, while besieging the "Place and For-
talico of Waughton," in January of that year, the said
slaughter having been committed by his son Andrew.
Nearly all of his surname in Haddingtonshire were concerned in this affair under Robert Hepburn, younger, of
Waughton, who was endeavoring to recapture his ancestral
house from the King's men. Haynes says George Hepburn was acquitted of intercommuning with Harry Hepburn
of Fortune, and Patrick Hepburn of Kirklandhill, then de-
nounced as rebels for being, like himself, adherents of their
Lord and Chief, James Hepburn, Earl of Bothwell and
Duke of Orkney. He was also found innocent of the charges
preferred against him.

George Hepburn had five sons, including Sir John, and
several daughters. He died before 1616, as in that year his
eldest son, also named George Hepburn, was "retoured in
the lands of Athelstaneford." Sir John Hepburn was born
about the year 1598 or 1600 at Athelstaneford. His kinsmen, the Hepburns of Waughton, since the days of the
Earl of Bothwell, had been under ban by the government
for various causes; and at the time when he left his home
for the camp, his uncle, John, the Knight, was at feud with
Douglas.

Young Hepburn is said to have been tall, active, powerful, and handsome in figure and face. His manners and bearing, when clad in the rich half armor of the period, were deemed eminently noble and commanding, bespeaking the decision of the soldier, mingled with the politeness of the courtier. He rode with skill and grace, and excelled in the use of the sword—a science at that time seduously cultivated among the Scottish gentry, for it was the weapon by which all disputes were settled, and to which all men of honor appealed. Col. Robert Munro, his friend, in his scarce and valuable work, "The Expedition," ever speaks of Hepburn with the highest praise. Being "comrades in danger," he says, "so being long acquainted, we were comrades in love—first at college, next in our travels in France."

Hepburn left school in 1614, but at what university he studied is uncertain. It is probable that he was the John Hepburn who studied at St. Leonard's College, St. Andrews, as that university was founded by one of his family, John Hepburn, Prior of the Augustinian Monastery, and son of Adam, second Lord Hailes. Many students of his name were studying there during the first twenty years of the seventeenth century. After leaving school he made a continental tour, and with his bosom friend Munro visited Paris and other places, studying the manners and languages of the countries through which they passed.

The rising fame of Gustavus Adolphus of Sweden, the hero of Protestantism in the Thirty Years War, attracted the attention of Sir John and "gave birth to a spark of military ardor within his breast, which was never extinguished till his death." Soon after his return home from the continent a path was opened to the military emulation of the Scots, by the spirited attempt which was made in the year 1620 to rescue the kingdom of Bohemia from the grasp of the house of Hapsburg. A Scottish regiment was being raised by Sir Andrew Gray, in 1620, and a camp was formed on a property of the Hepburns in East Lothian, near the village of

Athelstaneford. Hepburn joined the regiment. During the campaigns which followed, although only about twenty years of age, he so distinguished himself by his valor that he was given the command of a company in Colonel Gray's regiment.

JOINS GUSTAVUS ADOLPHUS.

After participating in many skirmishes and battles, and meeting with reverses, Gray left the regiment, when Hepburn conducted the survivors to Sweden and offered their services to Adolphus, who gladly accepted them. Inspired by the same ardor for military fame, his cousin, James Hepburn, heir apparent of the ancient house of Waughton, followed him to the Swedish wars, and was his companion in all their triumphs, toils, and dangers, amid which he soon attained the rank of lieutenant-colonel. The camp of Gustavus was then the military school of Europe. Sir John Hepburn, in the splendor of his arms and attire, outshone his comrades so far that he drew upon himself the reprehension of Gustavus—an affront which the haughty soldier never forgot.

In the year 1625 Gustavus appointed the young Captain Hepburn colonel of one of those auxiliary Bohemian regiments of which the First, or Royal Scots Regiment, of the British Line is now the direct representative. In this important command the young soldier, eager for adventure, burning for distinction, and impassioned for glory, acquitted himself with a valor and ability that few have equaled. Hepburn possessed, in an eminent degree, all those requisites necessary in the leader of soldiers of fortune—frankness and generosity, prudence or rashness, as the occasion required; with a strong power of perception and stratagem, instantaneous decision and action—all of which are so necessary to form the character of a great military commander. Every historian of the wars of Gustavus extols the brave Hepburn as the most famous of his cavaliers. An

old work, published at London in 1771, records that in 1633
two Scottish regiments were employed to guard the person
of Gustavus and the King of Bohemia, and he is said to
have ascribed his great victory at Leipzig to Hepburn's
Scottish brigade alone.

In the meantime Hepburn had been knighted for his
eminent services, and in the records of the time always appears as "Sir Iohn Habron." In the second campaign
against the Empire, the Swedish army was almost entirely
commanded by Scottish officers, and Hepburn's brigade was
generally known as the "Green Brigade," from the color of
their doublets, scarfs and feathers, and standards. In his
thirtieth year Hepburn found himself at the head of the
four best regiments of the Swedish army.

COMPLIMENTED BY THE KING.

Grant relates that after the great battle of Leipzig, Gustavus, accompanied by a glittering train of plumed cavaliers
and steel-clad general officers, rode up to Hepburn's iron
brigade, which was alike his right wing and right arm in
battle, at the head of which Hepburn was sitting on horseback sheathed in his magnificent armor. Dismounting, the
King approached on foot, and, while his face was lighted up
with admiration and respect for the courage and discipline
of Hepburn's soldiers, he made them a long address, com-
mending their conduct in the highest terms, and, thanking
them for their great share in winning the victory at Leipzig,
promised never to forget the debt he owed them.

The gallant Hepburn was still rising daily in the favor of
Gustavus, who found the impossibility of undertaking an
expedition of importance unaided by his able counsel, and
that dashing valor for which he was renowned throughout
the armies of Sweden, Austria, and afterwards of France,
and which won for him the reputation of being the best and
most fortunate soldier of the age.

In the campaigns on the Danube and the Rhine Hepburn's star always shone resplendent. When Munich was captured he was made military governor for a few days and established his headquarters in one of the grand old palaces of the city. Soon after this Gustavus, unfortunately for himself, quarreled with Sir John Hepburn, and during the altercation which ensued he upbraided Hepburn with his religion, (he was a Catholic,) and tauntingly referred to the extreme richness of his armor and apparel. This was a mortal insult to the brave soldier, and he never forgave Gustavus. The King was extremely sorry for his imprudent remark and apologized to Hepburn, but the latter could not be reconciled and announced his purpose to leave the service. After performing a few hazardous movements upon the urgent request of the King, he returned and approaching him said: "And now, sire," sheathing his rapier, "never more shall this sword be drawn in your service—this is the last time I will ever serve so ungrateful a prince!"

From this time the star of Gustavus entered on its decline. Luck seemed to forsake him, and in one month he fell in battle, shot through the head. The gallant Green Brigade was no longer present to protect him.

IN THE SERVICE OF FRANCE.

In the autumn of 1632, Hepburn and several other officers and soldiers bid farewell to the German wars and repaired to London. There he remained for some time, when he entered the service of Louis XIII. of France. His new commission as colonel is dated 26th January, 1633, and he also obtained the rank of *marechal-de-camp*, which invested the holder with the rank of a general officer, and was second only to a lieutenant-general. It was his duty to see the army properly disposed of in camp or quarters; to be present at all movements that were to be made; to be the first to mount his charger, and the last to quit him.

In France Hepburn soon gained the friendship and esteem of that wily diplomatist, Cardinal Richelieu. And in
his letters the Cardinal never mentions him without admiration, respect, and frequently affection. They had many in-
terviews on military and other matters of public importance, for Richelieu enjoyed his lively conversation, frank
manner, and his bold projects.

Hepburn's new Scottish regiment in the French service
was considerably above a thousand strong. In all French
works Hepburn's name is invariably spelled Hebron, and
sometimes Esbron, and his regiment was written Le Regiment d'Hebron. His first campaign was in Lorraine, and
though bearing the baton of a field marshal, he was only
thirty-six years old. And, as of old, success attended his
arms wherever he went. This gave so much satisfaction
that his regiment was ordered by Louis XIII. to take the
right of all others embodied. "The King has granted to
Colonel Hepburn," says Richelieu in a letter to Valette,
"the ransom of Metternich." This was an especial reward
for his distinguished services.

It would prove tedious to recount the many brilliant actions and encounters in which Hepburn and his soldiers
covered themselves with laurels while serving in Lorraine
during the spring of 1636, with the army under Bernard,
Duke of Weimar; but so eminent were his services, his valor
as a soldier, and skill as a leader, that Louis XIII. ordered
the diploma of a Marshal of France to be expedited under
his great seal, for *le Chevalier d'Hebron*, as he was named
at the court of Versailles.

KILLED AT SAVERNE.

Before Hepburn received from Paris his diploma of Marshal, he was ordered with his regiment of eight thousand
men to join the expedition against Saverne. The siege of
this stronghold proved very obstinate and there was much

hard fighting. The tall plume of Hepburn waved majesti-
cally in the thickest of the fight and inspired his soldiers
with courage. Having somewhat rashly volunteered to examine the principal breach in the walls, with his usual cool-
ness and temerity he approached too near, and at a time
when the strong batteries of the town and castle were firing
on the trenches with greater fury than ever. At that crisis,
a ball shot from the ramparts, either at random, or by some
musketeer whom the glitter of his rich armor had attracted,
struck the brave Hepburn in the neck, where his jointed
gorget failed to protect him, and he sank from his horse, to
be borne away by his faithful Scottish soldiers, a party of
whom immediately rushed forward to his assistance.

His fall was the signal for a fourth general assault, which
was successful, and with the familiar din of the distant strife
in his ears, Hepburn expired, with his unbuckled armor on,
his sword by his side, and the friends he loved—the comrades of his Bohemian wars, his Swedish and Bavarian
triumphs—standing sadly around him. He died like the
hero he had lived, in the blood-stained trenches, with the
Scottish standard drooping over him, and surrounded by
the dead, the wounded, and all the frightful debris of that
protracted siege, just as the sun set behind the mountains
of Alsace. His last words were touchingly expressive of
regret that he should be buried so far from the secluded
kirkyard where the bones of his forefathers lay.

GRIEF OF RICHELIEU.

Thus fell the brave soldier of fortune, ere the baton and
diploma, that would have made him a Marshal of France,
could reach the camp. It was on the 21st of July, 1636,
and when he was not more than thirty-eight years old.
When Richelieu was informed of his death, he replied in a
long and feeling letter, in which occur these sentences: "His
loss has touched me in so sensible and lively a manner that

it is impossible for me to receive any comfort. * * * I
have paid to his memory all the respect that lay in my
power, to express my value for him, ordering prayers to be
made to God for him, and assisting his nephew (George
Hepburn, of Athelstaneford,) with what he requires, as if
he were my son. The ransom of Metternich is secured to
him, and whatever is due to his uncle shall be most punc-
tually paid him."

All French military writers are lavish in extolling *le
Chevalier d' Hebron* as one who, to the most consummate skill
as a general, united the heroic courage of a soldier with
every good quality that could endear him to his comrades.
"Thus," says the historian of the British army, "terminated
the career of one of the best officers Scotland ever pro-
duced."

With his sword, helmet, spurs, and his Marshal's baton
laid on the coffin lid, his remains were borne, with every
mark of military respect, to the city of Toul, in Lorraine;
and there amid all the most imposing solemnities of the
Catholic church, his Scottish comrades, and his kinsmen,
George Hepburn, of Athelstaneford, and Col. Sir James
Hepburn, of Waughton, with the leading nobles and cheva-
liers of the French army, lowered him into the grave in the
southern transept of that magnificent cathedral that over-
looks the city; while in honor of high military rank and character, his worth and goodness, the bells tolled, the cannon
thundered from the ramparts, and the most solemn masses
were said by the Bishop for the repose of his soul.

Such was the respect borne him by the court of France
that many years afterwards a noble monument to his memory was erected by Louis XIV. above the place of his repose. It is still to be seen, says Grant, in the left transept
of the beautiful old church of Toul, and bears an epitaph
suitable to the worth of him who so deservedly was deemed

" the best soldier in Christendom, and consequently in the world."

HIS SUCCESSOR.

Marshal Hepburn was succeeded in the command of his regiment by Sir James Hepburn, heir apparent of the ancient estate of Waughton, who had served with him in Germany. He commanded *le Regiment d'Hebron* during the war in Alsace under Chatillon, and on the 16th of October, while fighting in the breach effected by blowing up a mine at Damvillers, a musket ball passed through his chest and he died from the effects of the wound November 7, 1637, nearly one year after his uncle's fall at Saverne. In 1639 the brothers and sisters of Sir John Hepburn laid claim as heirs to his estate to the Lord of Waughton. George Hepburn, son of the eldest brother of Sir John, who was then in France, did not sign the bond. The brothers and sisters having been confirmed as executors, collected twenty thousand pounds of a factor in Paris. This was probably the ransom of Metternich promised by Richelieu. Soon after this, says Grant, the family appear to have become extinct, or to have lost their lands, as there is in the Chancery Office a charter to Adam Hepburn de Hambie, Knight, of the lands of Athelstaneford.

EXCITING INCIDENTS.

In Domestic Annals of Scotland (Vol. I., p. 68,) an exciting incident of flight and escape is related. On the 7th of September, 1570, Robert Hepburn, second son of the Lord of Waughton, was a partisan of Queen Mary, although she was an exile in England. As he was traveling to visit his friends in Lothian, he was betrayed by a companion to the knowledge of a party of the Regent's friends, consisting of the Lords of Applegarth and Carmichael. They made an effort to arrest him, but he fled with such precipitancy to the Castle of Edinburgh, that he passed through the gate with his pursuers close behind him. At that time all those who adhered to the fortunes of the deposed Queen were in bad odor with the ruling power, and some of the Hepburns were under the ban, as this incident illustrates.

As an illustration of the violence of religious feeling which prevailed in those turbulent times, the same authority (Vol. I., p. 285,) relates that March 11, 1596, James Hepburn, of Moreland, and a young man named Birnie got into a dispute regarding the number of the sacraments. Hepburn strenuously asserted that there were seven, whilst Birnie as stoutly maintained that there were but two, "or else he would fight." Hepburn vehemently declared that he would defend his belief with the sword. They engaged in mortal combat and both were killed. Could religious fervor go further?

TAX COLLECTING IN EARLY TIMES.

According to the History of the Western Highlands, much difficulty was experienced in tax collecting, and some novel methods were resorted to. Sometime in 1605 Robert Hepburn, lieutenant of the King's Guard, was sent to the Isles to receive from the respective owners of the Castle of Dunygreg, in Isla, and Dorwart, in Mull, the amount of excise due. And in order to prevent the escape of the inhabitants of Kintyre and the West Isles, they were ordered by proclamation to deliver their boats to this officer, and at the same time they were prohibited from using boats without his special license. While the islanders were thus hemmed in the work of collection proceeded.

LAW AND LITERATURE.

It is stated in National Biography (Vol. XXVI.) that Robert Hepburn, born at Bearford, Haddingtonshire, in 1690 or 1691, early evinced such a talent for writing and study, that he was sent to Holland to acquire a knowledge of civil law. After finishing his studies he returned in 1711 to pursue the profession of the law in Scotland. Possessing such a taste for miscellaneous writing, he soon afterwards started a small periodical entitled *The Tattler*, by Donald McStaff, of the North. It soon became so satirical and personal that he was forced to suspend its publication at the end of the thirtieth number. Hepburn was admitted to the Faculty of Advocates in 1712, and died the same year. Although so young, he was the author of several books and pamphlets, and gave great promise of a brilliant career at the bar.

Sir George Buchan-Hepburn, son of John Buchan, of Letham, East Lothian, whose mother was Elizabeth, daughter of Patrick Hepburn, of Smeaton, was born March, 1739. He succeeded to the barony of Smeaton-Hepburn in 1764, and thereupon assumed the name and arms of Hepburn of Smeaton. In January, 1763, he was admitted a member of the Faculty of Advocates, Edinburgh, and from 1767 he was solicitor to the Lords of Session until 1790, when he was appointed Judge of the High Court of Admiralty, Scotland. On the 31st of December of the following year he was made Baron of the Exchequer. He retired in 1814, and May 6, 1815, was created a Baronet. Judge Hepburn was the author of "The General View of Agriculture and Rural Economy of East Lothian, &c.," in 1796. He died July 3, 1819. His first wife was Jane, eldest daughter of Alexander Leith, of Glenkurdy and Freefreld; and second, Margaret Henrietta, daughter of John Zacharias Beck, and widow of Brigadier-General Fraser, who fell at Saratoga. By his first wife he had an only son, who succeeded him in the baronetcy.

LEADER OF THE CAMERONIANS.

Burton informs us (Vol. VIII., pp. 162, 239, 388, note,) that some of the bold schemers of the period (1706) had arranged a plan for bringing the Cameronians and the Highlanders to act in concert. A fit man to lead them was found in Cunningham of Eckert, who had held the command of a regiment, and had heavy grievances against the government for disbanding it and leaving arrears of pay unsettled. He was to embody his Covenanting army at San-quhar, and at the same moment the Duke of Athole was to assemble the Jacobite Highlanders above the passes. Then the two armies were to march north and south until they met and then, with brotherly harmony, were to wheel round eastward to Edinburgh and disperse the Parliament. However well the Cameronians may have been prepared to guard their secrets, yet there was more than one man in their midst who gave their plans away.

Rev. John Hepburn, their choice leader, appears to have kept the government informed of what was contemplated. With a bold ingenuity, "acquired by his caustic studies, he justified his conduct on account of the importance of its consequences to the peace and stability of the country." His career as a priest had frequently been turbulent, and he had often been imprisoned. It is said in the pamphlets of the day that, although transferred from prison to prison, he managed to preach from his barred windows, "sometimes to a considerable congregation, consisting not entirely of stray passengers arrested by his uncouth earnestness, but containing some who had traveled from his own peculiar western district to drink at the fountain of Covenanted truth." "As yet," continues the narrative, "there has been no actual severance of this man from the church. He was under a sentence of separation, but it might be removed. He severed himself, however, from his friends and left the leadership that might naturally have been his, at this juncture, to another." This was the Rev. MacMillan, from whom a section of the Cameronians have sometimes been called MacMillanites; and his second in command was the Rev. McNeill.

MacMillan, like Hepburn, "was besieged by a battery of ecclesiastical prosecutions, which he treated with contempt." And as a result of this religious friction, it may be stated here, that on the 27th of July, 1712, the first secession from the Church of Scotland was organized, known as the Reformed Presbyterian Church.

In 1715 the Earl of Winton led the detachment from the Highland army. Meetings were held in his Castle of Seton, and it was among his followers that the first blood was drawn in the southern insurrection. The circumstances attending the affair were peculiarly painful. It was known that Rev. John Hepburn, of Keith, was preparing to join the Earl's standard, and as he was much respected by his neighbors, some of them proposed "by a sort of gentle violence, to prevent him from fulfilling his intentions by bringing him under the law which required suspected persons to find security to keep the peace." One morning, when it was learned that Hepburn had made preparations "for putting his foot in the stirrup," and he, "with his large family were assembled at breakfast, they were startled by the unwelcome vision of a party of the Royalist volunteers, headed by two of their own intimate friends, approaching the house. Hepburn refused to surrender—called to his party to mount, and was the first to fire. It is said that he fired in the air; but whether or not he may thus have endeavored to threaten without spilling blood is unknown, and his party charged. They were met by the fire of the volunteers, and Hepburn's youngest son, Robert, was shot dead!" In a temper little likely to disarm him of his hostility to the government, the bereaved father fled to the borders, where the general gathering was to commence.

The scheme of arrest, which was projected through friendship for Rev. John Hepburn, had a sad ending, as such schemes frequently have. It is regretted that the names of the other members of his family have not been preserved.

As his family is said to have been "large," it is likely that there were several sons. If their names were known they might clear away the uncertainty which obscures the ancestry of the members of the family which came to Northumberland, Pa.

A HERO OF WATERLOO.

Gen. Francis Hepburn, born August 19, 1779, was the second son (National Biography, Vol. XXVI.,) of Col. David Hepburn, of the 39th Foot and 105th Highlanders, who served at Belle Isle. His mother was Bertha Graham, of Inchbrakie, Perthshire, and he was a grandson of James Hepburn, of Brecartown and Keith, who spent his fortune in the Stuart cause. Francis was appointed an ensign in the 3d Foot Guards December 17, 1794, and rose rapidly. He served with his regiment in Ireland in 1798, and in Holland in 1799, and he was wounded badly at Cadiz in 1809. He joined Wellington in 1815, and was in temporary command of the 2d Brigade of Guards until the arrival of Sir John Byng, in May. He commanded his battalion at Quatre Bras and Waterloo. Soon after the battle commenced Hepburn was sent with the battalion and took command of the troops posted in the orchard of the chateau, an important service, the credit of which, by some official blunder, was given to a junior officer. The mistake was explained officially, but never publicly, and, it is said, was the means of depriving him of the higher honors awarded to other senior officers of the division of guards. He was made C. B., and had the fourth class decorations of the Netherlands Lion and St. Alexander Nevski in Russia. General Hepburn married, in 1821, Henrietta, eldest daughter of and co-heiress of Sir Henry Poole, last baronet of Poole Hall, Cheshire and Hook, Sussex, by whom he had two sons and a daughter. On the 10th of July, 1821, he was advanced to the rank of Major-General. He died at Tunbridge Wells June 7, 1835, aged 56 years.

Many members of the Hepburn family in early times sat in Parliament, and held offices of trust and responsibility. In "Collectanea Genealogica," (Vol. II., p. 178,) may be found a pretty full record of those who were favored in this respect.

HEPBURN ARMS.

The arms of Bothwell—James Hepburn,—as they appeared emblazoned above the stone chimney-piece, in the principal room of his castle, are described as follows:

Gules on a chevron, argent, two Scottish lions rending an English rose, (which had been the characteristic cognizance of Patrick Hepburn of Hailes, at the great battle of Otterburn,) quartered, azure with a golden ship; three chevronels on a field, ermine for the lordship of Soulis, with a bend azure for Vauss, lord of Dirltoun. His shield was supported by two lions guardant, and bearing on an escroll the motto: Keepe Tryste. This was originally written, *Kiip Trest*—Be Faithful.

For a description of the armorial bearings of a number of the heads of other Hepburn families, see Berry's Encyclopedia Heraldica, Vol. II. The following are given:

Hepburn of Smeaton, gules on a chevron between three martlets, argent, a rose between two lions passant, counterpassant of the first.

Hepburn of Humbie, gules on a chevron, a rose between two lions, combatant of the first.

Hepburn of Riccartown, gules on a chevron, argent, a rose between two lions combatant of the first, in base a buckle.

Hepburn of Blackcastle, the same, the buckle being argent, crest, a horse's head couped, proper garnished, gules.

Hepburn—place not given—gules on a chevron argent, a rose between two lions passant of the field, with a bordure ermine. Crest, a horse passant, argent, saddled and fastened by the bridle to a tree, under which he stands, all proper.

SAMUEL HEPBURN, AND HIS SONS, JAMES, WILLIAM, SAMUEL AND JOHN.

I. SAMUEL HEPBURN, father of James, William, Samuel and John, who settled on the West Branch of the Susquehanna River, Northumberland County, Pennsylvania, was born near Glasgow, Scotland, sometime in the year 1698. His remote ancestor was Patrick Hepburn, third Lord Hailes and first Earl of Bothwell. His immediate ancestor was Rev. John Hepburn, of Keith. He had several sons, it will be remembered, one of whom was killed under peculiar and painful circumstances. One of his sons was named James, known in history as the "Scotch patriot," and he became the father of Samuel. The latter named his eldest son James, and thus we have the line direct from the house of Keith.

For the truth of this statement we have living testimony. Mrs. Virgilia B. Brooke, of 1814 Tioga Street, Philadelphia, says : "My mother's sister, Juliana Grant, of Sunbury, Pa., married John Hepburn, of Northumberland. Many years ago, when I was reading the lives of the Pretenders to my father, the late Col. Kenderton Smith, of Philadelphia, he told me that James and John Hepburn, of Northumberland, were lineal descendants of James Hepburn of Keith, the Scotch patriot; that my uncle, John Hepburn, had stated this to him." No better testimony to establish the line of descent seems necessary.

The birthplace of Samuel Hepburn, near Glasgow, was

probably Bothwell Castle. Of his parentage, and how many there were in the family, and what his early advantages were, are unknown; but there is little doubt that the family was of high standing, that he received a good education, and moved in the best circles of Scottish society. What trade or occupation he followed is unknown, but it is believed that he was brought up to the mercantile business.

About 1746 he married Miss Janet ————, a Scottish lady, but nothing is known of her parentage and family. Soon after their marriage the young couple were forced to leave Scotland on account of religious persecution, having been brought up in the faith of the Covenanters, and they settled in Donegal, Ireland. At that time there was much feeling existing between the Catholics and Presbyterians, and it resulted in many of the latter abandoning their native land to seek homes in a country where they could enjoy their religious belief with impunity. It was this religious trouble which brought about the Presbyterian emigration to America, and the immigrants came to be known as Scotch Irish.

FAVORABLE REPORTS FROM AMERICA.

How long Samuel Hepburn and family were residents of Donegal we have no means of determining, but it must have been for many years, for all of his children were born there. When favorable reports reached him of the superior advantages to settlers in this country, they soon began to make an impression on his mind, and he yearned to know something more definite regarding them. His sons, James and William, therefore, determined to come to America and learn for themselves the true condition of affairs and report to their father. Early in 1773 they sailed from Londonderry and in due time landed at Philadelphia. At that time

James was twenty-six and William eighteen years of age. Soon after landing they started for the interior of Pennsylvania, being attracted by the reports which reached them of the beauty and fertility of what was known as the " New Purchase"—or more particularly the lands lying in the valley of the West Branch of the Susquehanna.

James, after familiarizing himself with the new country, and being satisfied of its future advantages, made his way back to Philadelphia, where he remained for fully ten years: but it is believed that in the meantime he made occasional return visits to the valley to look after the purchase of lands—or rather to locate tracts on which to place warrants. William, however, remained, and immediately became identified with the militia for the protection of the frontier against the inroads of the savages.

Having received encouraging reports from his sons in this country, Samuel Hepburn decided to emigrate also. He brought his younger sons, Samuel, Jr., and John, with him, and they undoubtedly all remained in and about Philadelphia, for we do not hear of them being on the Susquehanna until several years afterwards. Samuel was so old when he came to America that it seems doubtful if he engaged in any business during his life in this country. That he was a man of some means, and assisted his sons in their business operations, is probable.

STORY OF A SHIPWRECK.

When he became settled he determined to bring his wife and daughter to this country. The tradition, as related to the writer by a descendant (now deceased), is that he despatched his son John to Ireland for the purpose of settling up their affairs and then accompany them to America. His mission accomplished, they sailed from Londonderry on the ship Faithful Steward. The voyage proved uneventful until the coast of New Jersey was reached, when a storm arose and the vessel was driven on the sands and wrecked. An attempt was made to land a boat load of passengers, but it was swamped by the breakers, and Mrs. Hepburn and her daughter were drowned. Tradition says, furthermore, that the ladies might have been saved but for the additional weight of gold which they had belted around their persons.

There is a conflict of opinion, however, as to the time and place this calamity occurred. By some it is asserted that the wreck occurred off New Foundland; others maintain that it was on Absecom Beach, New Jersey, and about the year 1775. An officer of the Historical Society of Pennsylvania was recently informed from Atlantic City that the vessel was wrecked at Absecom in 1765. One boat load of passengers, in trying to get ashore, was swamped. They had with them a quantity of stamp act paper which the officers were anxious to get ashore, and it overloaded the boat. Much of this paper was afterwards picked up on the beach. From the wreck two sets of English china ware were saved, one of which is now at Atlantic City.

.The time given (1765) is probably an error. Doubtless 1775 was the year meant, as it is so easy to make errors in dates. This would harmonize with other events—especially with the arrival of James and William Hepburn, which was in 1772 or 1773.

There is another tradition, preserved by the Dougal family of Milton, Pa., which is that the vessel was lost off New Foundland. The father of the celebrated Dr. James Dougal was aboard the ship and was among the few saved. He reached land first, and succeeded in rescuing a young man who was in an exhausted condition. Edward Cooke and family—brother of Col. William Cooke, of Revolutionary fame—were among the lost. Dougal and Hepburn, it is claimed, were the first to arrive and impart the sad news to relatives and friends. This report was confirmed by his grandson, Jacob Cooke, of Muncy, Pa., (b. 1797), who died in 1887, and the account has been preserved by his daughter, Mrs. M. J. Levan, in her scrap-book, who distinctly remembers hearing it related by her father when a child. Unfortunately the year of this occurrence has not been preserved.

Both traditions are given for the benefit of all concerned, without any special attempt to reconcile them. It is possible that there were two vessels lost—the " Royal Stuart " and the " Faithful Steward," and both traditions may be correct. The Dougal tradition is that the vessel was named the Royal* Stuart. In that event the other vessel might have been wrecked earlier, as reported from Atlantic City.

However it may have been, the blow was a severe one, and cast a cloud of sorrow over the minds of the surviving relatives. At this time Samuel Hepburn must have been well advanced in years. No records of the ages of the lost have been preserved; neither is the name of the daughter remembered.

DEATH OF THE FATHER.

Soon after this great calamity fell upon Samuel Hepburn, he must have taken up his residence with his son James at Northumberland, and he did not long survive the crushing blow. The inscription on his marble headstone, in the cemetery at Northumberland, reads as follows:

In Memory of
SAMUEL HEPBURN,
Who Departed this Life
January 11th, 1795,
Aged 97 Years.

Almost one hundred years! By his side lie the remains of his sons, James and Samuel, and two grandsons. And within a few yards of their graves repose the ashes of the

*See sketch of Dr. James Dougal in Meginness' Biographical Annals, pp. 106–108, which was prepared by one of his descendants.

celebrated Dr. Joseph Priestley, discoverer of oxygen gas, who died February 6, 1801. There is something sublimely beautiful, as well as impressive, in the fact that almost side by side lie the mortal remains of the sturdy representative of an ancient Scottish house and the great English scientist, who electrified the world by his discovery; the frowning walls of Blue Hill rise in rugged grandeur but a short distance away, whilst the crystal waters of two rivers wash its eastern and southern base, and the receding hills, like ocean billows, roll away, adding beauty to the glorious natural scene which surrounds the place of their burial.

Samuel Hepburn and his wife Janet had issue:

2.   *i. James,* b. 1747; m. Mary Hopewell; d. January 4, 1817.
    ii. ———, daughter, lost by shipwreck.
3. *iii. William,* b. 1753; m. first, Crecy Covenhoven; second, Elizabeth Huston; d. June 25, 1821.
4. *iv. Samuel,* b. 1755; m. Edith Miller; d. December 24, 1801.
5.   *v. John,* b. 1757; m. Mary Elliott; date and place of death unknown.

JAMES HEPBURN AND FAMILY.

II. JAMES HEPBURN,[2] (Samuel,[1]) b. 1747, in Donegal, Ireland; d. at Northumberland, Pa., January 4, 1817, in the 71st year of his age. What his early advantages were are unknown, but that he received a sufficient education to fit him for business is shown by his eminent success in after life as a merchant and dealer in real estate. About 1773, in company with his brother William, he emigrated to America, sailing from Londonderry, and landed at Philadelphia. There, or in that vicinity, he appears to have remained about ten years. That he was engaged in the mercantile business seems certain, for on the 7th of May, 1781, he purchased an "out lot" at Northumberland, of John Lowden, for £140, and in the conveyance, which may be found on record at Sunbury, he is mentioned as a "merchant" of Philadelphia. His *first* purchase at Northumberland was a lot from Benjamin Allison, for £30, situated on North Way Street, containing a "two-story log house and tenement." The deed is dated April 18, 1781.

On the 17th of December, 1781, he married Mary, daughter of Daniel and Mary Becket Hopewell, of Mount Holly, New Jersey. The mother of his wife was a de Normandie, of France, and fled to England during the Huguenot persecutions, where she met and married Mr. Becket. They had two daughters, Mary and Elizabeth. The family tradition is that their parents did not come to this country, but the daughters came and lived with their uncle, Dr. John de Normandie, at Bristol, Pa. Mary married Daniel Hopewell, of Mount Holly, New Jersey, and her daughter, Mary, married James Hepburn, as stated above.

How long Mr. Hepburn remained at Mount Holly after his marriage is uncertain. Some claim that his eldest son, Samuel, was born there; others that he was born in Philadelphia.* Probably, while he was closing up his business in Philadelphia, with the intention of settling at Northumberland,—for we have seen that he had purchased real estate there before his marriage,—his wife remained at Mount Holly with her parents. The war had not then closed, and the Indians were still demonstrative in the vicinity of Northumberland, rendering it unsafe for two or three years afterwards for settlers along the river.

SETTLES AT NORTHUMBERLAND.

That James Hepburn had determined to settle at Northumberland there is no doubt, else he would not have made the investments he did. During his early visits to the valley of the Susquehanna his attention was attracted by the picturesque beauty of its scenery and the richness and fertility of its soil. He quickly perceived that the country possessed

---

*Dr. James Curtis Hepburn, LL. D., son of Samuel, and missionary to Japan, says that his father was born in Philadelphia, November 5, 1782. This should settle the matter beyond all dispute.

great natural advantages. At that time Northumberland, on account of its peculiarly eligible location at the junction of the North and West Branches of the Susquehanna River, promised to become a place of great commercial importance. It was laid out as early as 1772, and soon after attracted settlers of wealth and culture on account of its apparent advantages, and the natural grandeur and beauty of its surroundings.

The Revolution having ended, he soon decided what to do, and he entered into copartnership with John Cowden, and the firm of Hepburn & Cowden, dealers in merchandise, was organized. The year they commenced business is not clearly established. Hepburn's name first appears on the assessment books of Point Township (which included Northumberland) for the year 1787, which would indicate that he was there in 1786. The firm appears a year or two later. In 1787 he was assessed with "one house and lot, £400; two lots, £100; two out lots, £50; two horses and cows, £26; total valuation, £576." In 1788 he was assessed with "one servant, five years, £5." No "servant" appears afterwards on the assessments. The last assessment, made in 1816, the year before he died, is as follows: "Three houses, $1,500; store and wharf, $1,000; land on the river, $850; on the hills, $725."

PURCHASE OF HISTORIC LANDS.

The desire to acquire lands seems to have been one of the governing principles of James Hepburn. The records at Sunbury show that on the 5th of March, 1783, he purchased an out lot at Northumberland, of the Reuben Haines estate, containing 11 acres and 113 perches, for £90. September 7, 1785, lot of ground in Bald Eagle Township, of John Chatham, for £11.

By pre-emption warrant, dated September 3, 1785, he acquired a tract of land situated in what is known as Level

Corner, Lycoming County, called "Conquest," containing
191 acres and 67 perches. This tract he afterwards sold to
Robert Covenhoven, the famous Indian scout and Revolutionary soldier, for £310 15s. 8d., and the deed was made
August 11, 1790. It is a well known farm, and after passing
through several hands, is now owned by Jesse B. Carpenter.

By patent dated June 29, 1787, he became the owner of
the Antrim tract of 400 acres, situated on the east side of
Sinnemahoning Creek. The patent was signed by "His
Excellency Benjamin Franklin, Esq., President of the Supreme Executive Council," and the original is now in the
hands of Mr. A. D. Hepburn, a great-grandson, and resident
of Philadelphia. During the same month he also became
the owner of a tract of 403¾ acres situated on the head-
waters of Tangascootack, in what is now Clinton County, Pa.
Bituminous coal was discovered on this land at an early
day, and it is said that his heirs were the first to mine coal
and ship it to Marietta and Columbia by barges.

He also became the owner of 200 acres in District No. 3
of the "Depreciation Lands," on the Allegheny River. The
grant was originally made to William Stewart, who conveyed
the same to Hepburn, in fee, March 1, 1788. This land
laid west of Allegheny City.

On the 25th of April, 1788, he purchased 120 acres
of Thomas Pollock, for £85 14s. 3d. This land is described
as lying on Muddy Run, near the present town of Milton,
and Pollock's warrant was dated June 2, 1786. On the 7th
of April, 1787, he purchased 9 acres of David Hammond,
for £13 10s. This land was situated in Turbutt Township.

Once fairly under way, the mercantile firm of Cowden &
Hepburn evidently did a large business, and it was soon
recognized as one of the leading and substantial houses of
the county. Banking was also made a branch of their business, for on the 29th of September, 1790, the Hon. William
Wilson informed Governor Mifflin that he had drawn on him

for "fifty dollars specie" in favor of Hepburn & Cowden. This was for expenses incurred in the arrest of Samuel Doyle for being concerned with the Walker brothers in the killing of two friendly Seneca Indians, near the mouth of Pine Creek, in June, 1790, for boasting, while intoxicated, that they had killed and scalped the father of the Walkers near Northumberland, in 1783. Out of this tragedy grew an intricate land transaction. Benjamin Walker and his two brothers were forced to become fugitives to avoid arrest for killing the Indians in time of peace. Their father, John Walker, had pre-empted a tract of 292 acres and 142 perches, called Good Hope, east of the mouth of Pine Creek, in what is now Lycoming County. The heirs of John Walker sold this land in trust to James Hepburn, October 10, 1794, for £665. The conveyance was made by William Morrison, who was the husband of Sarah Walker, a sister of the Indian killers.*

May 4, 1791, William Marshall sold James Hepburn 200 acres of land in Pine Creek Township, for £100. This township is now embraced in Clinton County, Pa. The next purchase was a lot in Northumberland, of the Reuben Haines estate, for £25, on the 27th of September, 1797. It was called an out lot. The firm also owned several lots, and they had one in Lewisburg.

A GREAT LAND OPERATION.

In the largest purchase of lands James and William Hepburn were joint partners, and their *first* great contract was in the form of an agreement to purchase 600 acres of land lying on the rich alluvial plain north of the present borough of Montoursville, Lycoming County. The great mountain stream known as the Loyalsock runs west of this tract. Here the Wyckoff family, when they came from New Jersey, con-

---

*And it may be mentioned as a singular fact—after a lapse of one hundred years—that a portion of this tract (115 acres) now belongs to McClellan P. Hepburn, a great-grandson.

tracted for the purchase of a large body of land ; and it was
on this land that a bloody fight* with the Indians occurred
June 10, 1778, and Peter Wyckoff was taken prisoner and
carried into captivity.

And as the acquisition of this fine body of land marks
the beginning of the great land operations of the Hepburn
brothers, the article of agreement, drawn in the quaint English style of the time, is given in full.   It may be found in
Deed Book E, p. 118, Sunbury, and is as follows :

ARTICLE OF AGREEMENT made and concluded this
17th of March, 1779, between Peter Wychof of the one part,
and William Hepburn in equal partnership and in behalf of
and with his brother James Hepburn, all three of the Township of Muncy, County of Northumberland, and State of
Pennsylvania, witnesseth :

That for and in consideration of the purchase money
hereinafter mentioned, the aforesaid Peter Wychof hath
granted, bargained and sold, and by these presents doth
grant, bargain and sell unto the aforesaid William Hepburn
in partnership with his brother James as above described or
mentioned, a certain tract and parcel of land in the Township of Muncy, being part of his place he lately bought
of Andrew Stroup, described as follows : Beginning at a
marked elm, a corner of said tract, thence south 50 degrees
east 294 perches to a white oak, thence south 30 degrees
west 159 perches to a post, thence west 327 perches to a
post, thence north to the Mill Run,† thence up the same
the several courses and distances to the mouth of a certain
gut leading down from a post, the aforesaid elm corner,
thence up by the same to the place of beginning, supposed
to contain 600 acres and the usual allowances of six per
cent., be the same more or less, at £4 per acre, exclusive of
said allowance.

But if on inspection there should not be found within the
aforesaid limit 600 acres and allowances as aforesaid, that

---

* For a full account of that bloody affair and the misfortunes of the Wyckoff
family, see Revised History of the West Branch Valley, pp. 537–9.

† Now known as Mill Creek.

then it shall be made up by starting at the mouth of the said gut where it empties into the aforesaid Mill Run, and from thence cutting off as much of the lower end of the remainder of said Wychof's tract as will make up 600 acres and the usual allowances. And the said William Hepburn's heirs, &c., or either of them, is to pay said Peter Wychof, his heirs, &c., or assigns, the first payment to wit: £1000 current money on or before the first day of March next, at which time Peter Wychof, his heirs, &c., is to make two sufficient deeds for said tract clear of all encumbrances—the Proprietaries quit rents accruing hereafter excepted—to said William Hepburn and his brother James, their heirs, &c., according as they may see fit to divide said tract, they giving bonds for the remainder of said purchase money, the one half of which is to be paid on or before the 1st day of November next, and the other half against the 1st day of May in the year 1780. Both of the aforesaid payments in current money; and also at the payment of the £1000, the said Peter Wychof, his heirs, &c., to deliver up quiet and peaceable possession of the aforesaid premises to the said William and James Hepburn, their heirs, &c., free from any let, hinderance or interruption from him or any by or under him on any pretence whatsoever. In the true performance of all and every the above articles and agreements each of the said parties have bound themselves to each other, on failure thereof, in the penal sum of £4,800 like money aforesaid.

In testimony whereof the parties have hereunto inter-changeably set their hands and seals the day and year first above written.

PETER WYCHOF.
WILLIAM HEPBURN.

Signed, sealed and delivered in the presence of James Covenhoven and Andrew Culbertson.

NORTHUMBERLAND COUNTY, TO WIT:

Before me the subscriber, one of the Justices of the Court of Common Pleas in and for the County aforesaid, on the 13th day of May, in the year of our Lord 1788, personally appeared Peter Wychof in the above deed of bargain and sale mentioned, and acknowledged the same to be his act and deed and desired it might be recorded as such. Witness my hand and seal the same day and year.

Jos. J. Wallis.*

I do hereby acknowledge that I have received of James Hepburn by the hands of my wife Rebecca Wychof £1000 on account of within articles, the same bearing date September 26, 1779, as witness my hand and seal this 20th day of April, 1785.

Peter Wychof.

Recorded 28th day of February, 1791.

THE FIRST DEED.

The first deed under the terms of the article of agreement was made August 29, 1788, and may be found in Deed Book E, p. 117, Sunbury, Pa. It is as follows :

This Indenture made the twenty ninth Day of August in the Year of our Lord one thousand seven hundred and eighty eight, Between Peter Wyckof of the County of Northumberland in the Commonwealth of Pennsylvania Yeoman of the one part and James Hepburn of the same place, merchant, of the other part. Whereas a certain Andrew Stroup of the County aforesaid by his certain Indented Article did agree to sell and convey to the said Peter Wyckoff, for the Consideration therein mentioned, all that Tract, piece or parcell of Land, in the County aforesaid, lying and being Eastward of the Main Branch of the Loyal Sock Creek, be the same more or less, the quantity thereof being yet unascertained, being part of a larger Tract, contracted for and bargained by the said Stroup with a certain Turbut Francis late of the City of Philadelphia, Esquire, now deceased—situate on Loyal Sock Creek aforesaid, containing in the whole 1019 acres and 154 Perches, as the same is described by metes and bounded in the said article, which article is dated February 26th, 1778.

*Under the Constitution of 1776, Joseph Jacob Wallis was commissioned a Justice, November 2, 1787, to serve for seven years. He was a half-brother of the celebrated Samuel Wallis, owner of the Muncy Farms (now Halls), situated a short distance east of the Wychoff tract. He married a daughter of John Lukens, Surveyor General of Pennsylvania, and their son, John Lukens Wallis, was the first white male child born west of Muncy Creek, in 1773.

And Whereas the abovenamed Peter Wyckoff by an article sealed, or deed poll, dated March 17th, 1779, for the consideration therein mentioned, did grant, bargain and sell to a certain William Hepburn and James Hepburn party hereto, as by the same article, bounded and butted, the same may appear, a certain part, parcel or portion of his share of the aforesaid 1019 acres and 154 perches, divided therefrom by the main Branch of Loyal Sock Creek, lying eastwardly thereof, which said parcel of Land so sold by the said Peter Wyckoff to the said William Hepburn and James Hepburn is supposed to contain six hundred acres be the same more or less.

Now This Indenture Witnesseth, that the said Peter Wyckoff in consideration of the sum of two hundred and fifty pounds lawful money of Pennsylvania to him in hand paid by the said James Hepburn, the Receipt whereof is hereby acknowledged, hath given, granted bargained and sold to the said James Hepburn, his heirs and assigns all his, the said Peter's Right, Title, Interest, Use, Property, Possession, Claim or Demand whatever, either at law or in Equity, of in and to, all his Residue or reserved share of the said great Tract of 1019 acres and 154 Perches, divided therefrom by the main Branch of Loyal Sock Creek and lying eastwardly thereof, not heretofore conveyed by the said last recited article or deed poll to the said William Hepburn and James Hepburn, be the quantity thereof more of less. To have and to hold to the said James Hepburn, his heirs and assigns, all his title, Possession, or Right of Possession of the whole or any part of the said before described Tract of land, be the same more or less, lying eastwardly of the main Branch of Loyal Sock Creek, together with all and singular the appurtenances, Papers and writings whatever, the Reversions and Remainders and the Rents, Issues and Profits thereof— (saving to William Hepburn all his lawful Right and claim by and under the last above recited article) to the only proper use, benefit and behoof of the said James Hepburn, his heirs and assigns forever. And the said Peter, for himself his heirs, Executors and Administrators doth covenant, grant and agree to and with the said James Hepburn, his heirs and assigns that he and they shall and will, at all times hereafter, at the cost and charges of the said James Hepburn,

his heirs and assigns, make and execute such further or
other acts, deeds or assurances in law, as may be thought
necessary by his or their counsel learned in the law, to vest
a full and entire fee simple in the said hereby granted premises in the said James Hepburn, his heirs and assigns forever.

In Testimony whereof the said Parties to these Presents
have hereunto interchangeably set their hands and seals the
Day and Year first before written.

PETER WYCKOF, [L. S.]

Sealed and Delivered in the presence of
    WM. HEPBURN,
    ROBERT HUSSTON.

It would require several pages to enumerate all the tracts
of land that he owned or was interested in, at one time or
another, in Lycoming and Northumberland counties. The
records show that in 1796 he was assessed with 8,000 acres
of "unseated lands" on the head-waters of Mill Creek, in
the former county, and the firm of Hepburn & Cowden
with 200 acres "five miles up Lycoming Creek."

A FREQUENT VISITOR.

Although making his headquarters in Philadelphia for
ten years, the public records show that James Hepburn was
a frequent visitor to the valley of the West Branch, called
there no doubt in the interest of his brother, who was an
active participant in military operations. Under date of
December 2, 1777, we find him, in connection with William,
signing a petition* of the inhabitants of Muncy Township,
Northumberland County, to the Supreme Executive Council,
praying that they be provided with another magistrate.
Muncy Township at that time embraced the great tract of
land of which they [the Hepburns] afterwards became the
owners.

They also united with the inhabitants of Muncy Township, under date of June 10, 1778, in a petition† to the Su-

---

*Vide Hist. Lycoming Co., p. 111.
† Vide Hist. Lycoming Co., p. 144.   Ibid. 169.

preme Executive Council of Pennsylvania, setting forth the
great good done by Colonel Brodhead's regiment while it
was stationed at Fort Muncy, by holding back the savages,
and earnestly praying Council to take the necessary steps
to have that regiment, or some other body of Continental
troops, stationed among them.

That James Hepburn had the confidence of the authorities is shown by the fact that early in 1779 Colonel Hunter,
stationed at Fort Augusta (Sunbury), and serving as County
Lieutenant, entrusted him with the delivery of an important
letter to the Supreme Executive Council, in Philadelphia,
relating to the necessity of medical supplies for the "poor
wounded men," and he was instructed to impart "other
points of information not alluded to in the correspondence."

VOLUNTEERS IN A MILITARY COMPANY.

Soon after locating at Northumberland he became a
member of Capt. John Lowdon's company of "Northumberland Volunteers," which marched to suppress the riot
at Wyoming (now Wilkes-Barre), August 4, 1784.* This
was caused by the ill feeling existing between the Connecticut and Pennsylvania settlers regarding land titles, and the
militia were sent there by order of the Supreme Executive
Council, Sheriff Antes being unable to suppress the disturbance. The expedition had a lively time at Wyoming.
Quiet was finally restored, and several of the ringleaders
were arrested, brought to Sunbury and imprisoned.

IDENTIFIED WITH THE CHURCH.

Having been brought up in the faith of the Covenanters,
he always took a deep interest in church affairs. On the
31st of May, 1787, he became a signer, as deputy from
Northumberland, of the call for Rev. Hugh Morrison, from

* This date would indicate that he was there early in 1784, but probably
had not yet brought his family.

the united congregations of Buffalo, Sunbury and Northumberland, to the Carlisle Presbytery. In this call it was stated that, "having never in these parts had the stated administration of the Gospel Ordinances; yet highly prizing the same, and having a view to the advancement of the Kingdom of Christ, and the spiritual edification of ourselves and families, have set ourselves to obtain that blessing among us." The appeal was granted by the assignment of Mr. Morrison to the charge.

The first meeting of the Northumberland Presbytery was held in the Presbyterian Church, Northumberland, the first Tuesday of October, 1811. There were a number of distinguished ministers present, and James Hepburn appeared as one of the four elders, and took part in the organization.

DISSOLUTION OF THE FIRM.

The firm of Hepburn & Cowden, as merchants, did a large business. In the issue of Kennedy's *Gazette* for April 16, 1794, they published an advertisement offering a reward of fifty dollars for the apprehension of certain "malicious, evil disposed persons," who on the 30th of March previously had rolled upwards of one hundred bushels of salt, one wagon, and one cart from their landing into the river, and cut loose a boat.

Soon after the firm was fairly under way they secured a large stone warehouse in Lewisburg, Pa., which they used in connection with their commercial business, and more particularly for the storage of grain purchased from the farmers of Buffalo Valley. This grain, which was shipped to market in arks at that time, was held in the storehouse until the stage of water in the river warranted the starting of these vessels on their voyages. As late as 1798 the old firm seems to have occupied this warehouse as tenants.

The firm finally dissolved June 4, 1794, after having been in existence about ten years, and both members continued business individually. John Cowden was appointed the first postmaster on the establishment of the office in 1795, and served until January 12, 1837, a period of about forty-two years, when he died, having survived his old partner twenty years. James Hepburn, after the dissolution of the firm, conducted his store in a log building on the corner of North Way and Duke Street. Some idea of the mercantile business of that time may be formed from the following enumeration of articles in an advertisement inserted in the *Gazette*, in 1801, by James Hepburn:

Superfine, second, and coarse cloth, mixed, plain, striped, and white cassimeres; striped, plain, blue and brown nankeens; chintzes, calicoes, ging-mufflins, and dimities of all kinds, large and small umbrellas, velvets, thickset and fancy cords, satin, lustrings, Persians, and Sarsonets, calimancoes, moureens, taboeens and durants; Irish linens, checks, and bed ticks, iron and copper tea kettles, German and cradling scythes; sugars, coffee, and tea of almost all kinds, sherry, madiera, and port wines, Jamaica spirits, French brandy, with a few barrels of old whiskey, best Spanish and American cigars, with a number of other articles.

Several articles are mentioned in the above list which are unknown by the names given them by the old merchant to-day, whilst there are several others whose names have not changed during the lapse of years. How long Mr. Hepburn continued in active business as a merchant is unknown, but it must have been until near the close of his life in 1817. As his age was not so great as to prevent him from taking an active part, and evidently being a man of strength, push and energy, it is likely that he looked after his affairs almost to the last.

APPOINTED A JUSTICE IN 1796.

On the 14th of March, 1796, Governor Thomas Mifflin appointed James Hepburn a Justice of the Peace for the township of Point, which included the town of Northumberland. The commission, which is on record at Sunbury,

(Deed Book H, p. 399,) ends with these words : " So long as you shall behave yourself well." How long he served is unknown, but it is safe to conclude that on account of his business qualifications and the methodical training of his mind, he made a good Justice and " behaved " himself " well."

MORE LAND HISTORY.

We now return to the consideration of the purchase of the large tract of land which James and William Hepburn had agreed to make from Peter Wyckoff in 1788. The terms of the contract were not fully carried out until April 9, 1803, when Peter Wyckoff and his wife Rebecca, (Deed Book F, p. 78, Williamsport,) in consideration of £2,400, conveyed the land to James and William Hepburn. The deed, which is very long, recites the history of the title in full, and in view of its historical importance a very full brief is herewith given :

On the 3d of April, 1775, Turbutt Francis entered into an agreement with Andrew Stroub to convey by deed on or before the 1st of May following said tract of land founded on patent from the Proprietaries. Said tract was surveyed in pursuance of an application, No. 16, entered February 4, 1769, by Samuel Purviance, who by deed dated July 4, 1773, conveyed the land to Turbutt Francis in fee. Francis died intestate without executing a deed to Stroub ; but by his will, dated February 11, 1777, appointed his wife Sarah and Samuel Mifflin his executors, and authorized them to sell any part of his real estate they might judge proper. Mifflin soon afterward died, and Sarah in the meantime married John Connelly, and in November, 1797, she petitioned the court of Northumberland County for leave to execute a deed to Stroub, which was granted. The Commonwealth of Pennsylvania had by letters patent dated March 18, 1796, granted and confirmed the land to Sarah Connelly, surviving executor of the said Turbutt Francis. On the 16th of May, 1798, she conveyed the tract supposed to contain 1,000 acres to the said Stroub in fee. It was afterwards discovered that there was an error in the survey mentioned and recited in

the patent, when the parties agreed to destroy the deed,
which was done. An order of the Board of Property, dated
July 9, 1799, authorized a warrant of re-survey to issue to
correct the error. Before this was done Sarah Connelly
died, but she left a will bearing date November 3, 1795,
wherein she appointed Samuel Mifflin and Mathias Harrison
her executors. The latter refused to act, whereupon letters
testamentary were granted to Mifflin. It appeared that the
said Sarah Connelly, by a deed (intended) dated December
21, 1799, had conveyed the land unto the said Samuel Mifflin,
and he by deed dated March 27, 1801, conveyed the tract
to Stroub, which contained 999 acres and 167 perches—it
being the same tract for which the Commonwealth had
granted a patent dated September 27, 1800. Stroub and
his wife Mary, therefore, under date of June 30, 1801, conveyed to Peter Wyckof 880½ acres, it being part of the
tract of 999 acres and 167 perches before referred to. Wyckof, in consideration of the sum mentioned above, conveyed
the same, under date of April 9, 1803, to James and William
Hepburn, together with all the buildings, improvements,
water courses, rights, etc. The deed was duly signed by
Peter Wyckof and his wife Rebecca, and executed and
delivered in the presence of James Stewart and Peter Van-
derbelt.

It took a long time and the "use of much red tape" to
obtain a clear title to this splendid piece of land, but it was
finally accomplished. In after years it came to be known as
the "Charles Lloyd* Farm," and it may be better designated

---

*Charles Lloyd was the son-in-law of John and Frances Hollingsworth,
having married their daughter Susannah. Mr. Hollingsworth died intestate
in the early part of this century, and the estate came into possession of his
widow. Under date of January 21, 1835, (Will Book A, p. 279,) she bequeathed
the farm to her son-in-law and daughter, with the injunction that they were to
retain it in "the family and not to sell or dispose of any part thereof." She
was a sister of Lydia, wife of Samuel Wallis, who once owned the Muncy,
now known as Halls Farms, and she willed $100 each to Hannah Miller and
Cassandra Smith, surviving daughters of Mrs. Wallis. Among other bequests
was a gold watch to each of her grandsons, and a dozen silver table and teaspoons to each of her granddaughters. As the will was filed for probate February 3, 1837, she died in the latter part of January of that year.

now by stating that the paper mill stands on it. The land to-day is worth over $150 per acre; it cost the Hepburns £2,400, " Pennsylvania currency."

A SHREWD EXCHANGE.

The next movement on the part of these sagacious brothers was one that involved a great deal, although they never imagined for a moment what the future result would be— the growth of a rich, flourishing and enterprising city of forty thousand inhabitants. They doubtless contemplated some benefits to be derived from their enterprise, yet nothing like what was developed half a century after they had passed away.

Among the early land owners in what is now Lycoming County was John Hollingsworth, a Quaker from Philadelphia. He had become the possessor of two tracts of land lying east of Lycoming Creek. The Hepburn brothers conceived the idea of proposing to exchange an equal quantity of their Loyalsock land for the Hollingsworth tracts. What their object may have been is unknown, as their land was more beautifully situated and much richer for agricultural purposes, but future developments show that in the end the Hollingsworth land became of immense value. Hollingsworth accepted their proposition to exchange for a nominal consideration, and as his deed is of very great historical importance, locally considered, it is given in full. It may be found in Deed Book F, page 74, Williamsport, and is as follows:

MOUNT JOY AND DEER PARK.

This indenture made the third day of March, 1804, between John Hollingsworth, of Muncy Township, Lycoming County and State of Pennsylvania, gentleman, and Frances his wife, of the one part, and James Hepburn of Northumberland Town and County, esquire, and William Hepburn, of Loyalsock Township, Lycoming County, esquire, of the other part, witnesseth:

That whereas the late Proprietaries of Pennsylvania, by their patent bearing date the 4th day of April, 1772, granted and confirmed to John Nisbett in fee a certain tract of land called "Deer Park," situated on the north side of the West Branch of the Susquehanna, in the county of Northumberland, now Lycoming, which said patent is founded upon an application in the name of John Nisbett, dated the 3d of April, 1769, and numbered 734 in the lottery of that date, as by the said patent recorded in the Roll's office of the Commonwealth of Pennsylvania, in Book AA, vol. 13, p. 80, more fully and at large appears;

And whereas the same John Nisbett by the name Maxwell Nisbett, by his indenture dated the 16th day of April, 1772, granted and conveyed the aforesaid tract of land to Turbutt Francis in fee, as by the said indenture of record in the office for recording deeds in Northumberland County, in Book D, p. 391, more fully and at large appears;

And whereas the late Proprietaries of Pennsylvania by their patent bearing date the 2d of June, 1772, granted and conveyed to Turbutt Francis and his heirs a certain tract of land called "Mount Joy," situated then in Northumberland County, now in Loyalsock Township, Lycoming County, and lying on the north side of the West Branch of the Susquehanna, adjoining the before mentioned tract called "Deer Park," which said patent is founded on an application in the name of Robert Galbraith, dated the 3d of April, 1769, and number 1823 in the lottery of that date, which said Robert Galbraith, by deed poll dated the 27th day of March, 1770, granted and conveyed the said application and land surveyed, or to be surveyed thereon, to Turbutt Francis in fee, as by the said patent enrolled in the Roll's office of Pennsylvania, in Book AA, vol. 13, p. 145, more fully and at large appears;

And whereas the said Turbutt Francis being so seized in his demesne as of fee of the two before mentioned tracts called "Deer Park" and "Mount Joy," made his last will and testament dated the 11th day of February, 1777, duly authenticated to pass real estates, and remaining in the Register's office at Philadelphia, by which will he appointed his wife, Sarah Francis, and his father-in-law, Samuel Mifflin, his executors, with power to sell all and every part of his estate as they might judge proper; and the said Turbutt

Francis afterwards died and the said executors proved the
will and took upon themselves the execution thereof, but
the said Samuel Mifflin soon after dying, the said Sarah
Francis was left sole executrix ;

And whereas the said Sarah Francis in pursuance of the
powers granted to and vested in her by said will granted
and conveyed the two aforesaid tracts of land called " Deer
Park " and " Mount Joy," along with the other land, to
Tench Coxe in fee by indenture bearing date the 2d day of
May 1782, as by said indenture of record in the office of the
Recorder of Deeds in Northumberland County, in Book F,
p. 169, more fully and at large appears ;

And whereas the said Tench Coxe by indenture dated
the 8th of September, 1784, granted and conveyed the aforesaid two tracts of land, with other lands, to Jonathan Mifflin
in fee, as by the said indenture recorded in the office of the
Recorder of Deeds of the County of Northumberland in
Book E, p. 27, more fully and at large upon reference being
thereunto had will appear ;

And whereas the said Jonathan Mifflin by his indenture
bearing date the 29th day of April, 1786, granted and conveyed the aforesaid tracts of land called " Deer Park " and
" Mount Joy" to John Hollingsworth and his heirs and
assigns, as by the said deed of record in the office of the
Recorder of Deeds in Northumberland County, in Book D,
p. 392, more fully and at large upon reference being thereunto
had will appear.

Now this indenture witnesseth, that John Hollingsworth
and Frances his wife, for and in consideration of the quantity
of 600 acres of land situate in Muncy Township, Lycoming
County, conveyed to him, the said John Hollingsworth,
in fee by the aforesaid James Hepburn and William Hepburn ; and in consideration of the sum of five shillings to
him in hand paid at or before the execution and delivery of
this indenture, the receipt whereof is hereby acknowledged,
have granted, bargained, &c., to the said James Hepburn
and William Hepburn, and their heirs, as tenants in common
and not as joint tenants, those two several tracts or parcels
of land before mentioned to wit :

Deer Park, beginning at a post on the bank of the West

Branch of the Susquehanna, thence by land surveyed for the Proprietaries, now John Rose's land, north 255 perches to a stone, thence by land surveyed to Robert Galbraith east 215 perches to a stone, and south 222 perches to a post on the bank of the West Branch of the Susquehanna aforesaid; thence up along the said bank 230 perches to the place of beginning, containing 311 acres and allowances of six per cent. for roads and highways;

And also all that tract called Mount Joy, beginning at a post at the side of the aforesaid West Branch of the Susquehanna, thence by the last described tract called Deer Park north 222 perches to a stone, and west 215 perches to a stone, thence by lands now of John Rose north 100 perches to a stone, thence by Sim's land east 315 perches to a marked pine, thence south 272 perches to a marked ash on the bank of the West Branch of the Susquehanna aforesaid, thence up the same the several courses thereof to the place of beginning, containing 300 acres and allowances, &c., together with all and singular the rights, liberties, privileges, &c., of the said John Hollingsworth, &c., unto the said James and William Hepburn and their heirs, assigns, &c., as tenants in common and not as joint tenants.

The above deed was signed March 3, 1804, by John Hollingsworth and wife in the presence of Samuel Harris, J. P., and Charles Huston, Esq., attorney, by whom it was probably drawn. This completed the exchange, but in order to make the line of title complete and legal beyond peradventure, James and William Hepburn executed a deed in consideration of five shillings and 600 acres (Deed Book D, p. 333,) of land lying on the Loyalsock to Hollingsworth. Next in order came the division of the Deer Park and Mount Joy tracts between the brothers by a deed of partition, (Deed Book I, p. 250, Williamsport,) executed September 6, 1810. In this division William took the Deer Park tract, lying between what are now Campbell and Susquehanna streets; and Mount Joy, lying between Campbell and Hepburn streets, fell to James. Several years before the deeds were executed, however, each one had occupied the land and made improvements, showing that the exchange and division had long been contemplated.

These two tracts of land now constitute the central part of the city of Williamsport, and many of the most elegant residences and churches are found on Third and Fourth streets, which run east and west. The first saw mill sites were sold off the Mount Joy tract along the river; and in course of time the great mills extended over the lower part of the Deer Park land also. That section became the great manufacturing district, and continues so to-day, but the two brothers had been in their graves forty years before this industrial development began to manifest itself on the land they once owned. Nearly all their land has long since been covered with buildings, and with the improvements is now worth several millions of dollars.

On the 12th of October, 1807, James Hepburn purchased a tract of 213 acres lying on Larry's Creek, Lycoming County, at a sale held by Sheriff Cummings, as the property of Henry Thomas. He had erected iron works on the land and carried on business extensively for several years, but meeting with reverses was forced to the wall. He held this farm until April 2, 1812, when he sold it to John Knox for $6,000. Knox was a native of Scotland and a lineal descendant of the celebrated Reformer of the same name. He built a mill on the property and made other improvements, which greatly enhanced its value. Mr. Knox lived there until his death, which occurred October 18, 1854, in the 88th year of his age.

WILL OF JAMES HEPBURN.

The will of James Hepburn, which is on record at Sunbury, (Book 2, p. 315,) is a concise and businesslike document, typical of the man; and as it is important in connection with his history, it is given in full:

This is the last will and testament of me, James Hepburn, of the town and county of Northumberland, in the State of Pennsylvania, Esq.

First. I will that all my debts and funeral expenses be paid and discharged.

Secondly. I devise to my executors all estate, real and personal, to be by them disposed of as in hereafter directed, that is to say: Let my present wife, Mary Hepburn, possess and enjoy the house and lot we now occupy in the town of Northumberland, together with all the furniture, utensils, plate, china, linen, books and liquors as they may be found at the time of my decease; and also two cows, the poultry and hogs that I may be possessed of at the time of my decease; also my out lot in the town of Northumberland, usually known as the "orchard lot." All these are to belong to her during the time of her natural life, and at her decease the house, lot, furniture, and such utensils, plate, china, linen, books and live stock as remain, to revert to my executors as part of my estate to them devised. I also will that my said wife be paid $300 immediately after my decease for her comfortable maintenance until my executors can make arrangements for the speedy and regular payment of her annuity hereafter directed. I also will and require my executors to pay to my said wife an annuity of $600 annually during her natural life by quarterly payments, to be computed from three calendar months after the day of my decease.

Item. I will that my executors do pay $100 annually to my wife, Mary Hepburn, for the support of her mother, Mary Eldredge,* so long as she shall continue to reside with my said wife; but if she shall choose in preference to reside with any of my children, who may be willing to maintain and provide for her, then the said annuity of $100 yearly shall be paid to such child.

Item. Let my executors keep fair and regular accounts of all the rents, issues, profits and proceeds of all my real estate to be by them received until my houses, lots and tracts of land, improved and unimproved, shall be sold and

---

* Her name by the first marriage was Hopewell, but having married again it became Eldredge. She died November 10, 1816,—less than two months before Mr. Hepburn,—in the 80th year of her age, and is buried at Northumberland, in the Hepburn lot.

disposed of, which I hereby authorize my said executors to
do, leaving it to their discretion to sell and dispose of to
the best advantages, according as circumstances may require
and induce them. I would have my unimproved lands sold
first, and the whole to be sold within ten years from the
day of my death, or so soon after the ten years as possible,
not to make too great sacrifice of the property if the time
should then happen to be unfavorable for the purpose.

Item. I will that my executors do collect speedily all my
personal property and all debts due to me and keep an
account of the same.

Item. My personal property and the rents, issues, profits
and proceeds of sale from time to time of my real estate
being thus collected shall form an aggregate fund out of
which this bequest of my last will shall be paid and discharged.

Item. As my sons, Samuel, Andrew, James and John,
will at my decease have received a good part of their portion
in advance, let them be made debtors to the said aggregate
fund each in $1,000.

Item. My will is that all my male children who may be
minors at the time of my decease shall be allowed $200 a
year to support them until they become of age ; and all my
minor female children $150 a year to support them until
they become of age or are married.

Item. After paying my debts and funeral expenses and
the annuities to my wife and my mother-in-law, Mary
Eldredge, and the sums hereinbefore appropriated for the
maintenance and education of my minor children, my will
is that the rents, issues, profits and proceeds of my estate,
real and personal, shall from time to time be equally divided
amongst all my children, male and female, the share of them
as are not of age, to be invested by my executors for the
benefit of such minor children respectively until they become
of age or are married.

Item. On the decease of my wife, Mary Eldredge, or any
of my children who may happen to die under age, unmarried
and without lawful issue, the annuities, portions and bequests
hereinbefore to them, or either of them, respectively made,
shall lapse, revert and become a part of the aggregate fund

of my estate. But if any of my children should die leaving lawful issue, let the share of the parent be by my executors invested for the benefit of such lawful issue in equal proportion, and become payable when such of my grandchildren as may be deprived of their parent shall become of age or are married.

Item. I appoint my sons, Samuel, Andrew and James, joint executors of this my last will and testament, hereby authorizing them, or the majority of them, to act in all things necessary to carry my said will into execution.

[Signed]   JAMES HEPBURN.

June 23, 1812.

Witnesses: John Cowden, Samuel McClintock.

The will was probated January 22, 1817, in the office of the Register at Sunbury, Pa., the testator having died January 4, 1817. He was buried at Northumberland, and in the new cemetery his tombstone may now be seen by the side of that of his father.

Thus passed away one of the most active and successful business men of his time at the almost exact age of threescore and ten. He died in the full faith of his immediate ancestors, never having relaxed in the least from the belief that was taught him by his parents, who had to leave their native land and fly to Ireland, because of their belief in the doctrines of the Presbyterian Church.

Through life Mr. Hepburn adhered to many of the customs of his forefathers, and was a typical representative of his ancient family. There is a tradition that he "kept his coach and four," and often drove in that style from Northumberland to Williamsport when he went there on business, or to visit his brother, Judge William Hepburn.

The concise wording of his will shows that he possessed a methodical mind, and was trained to despatch business with clearness and precision. No point or suggestion for the settlement of his large estate was omitted, and all his family and heirs were remembered and provided for. The fact that his three eldest sons were chosen as his executors shows that he had full confidence in their ability and integrity to administer his estate fairly and honestly, and the final settlement showed that he was correct in his conclusions.

His wife, Mary Hopewell Hepburn, survived him nine years, and died at Williamsport May 1, 1826, aged 65 years. Soon after the death of her husband she moved to Williamsport, where, with her unmarried children, she lived in a house adjoining that of her son, Andrew D., which had been built for her. It stood on Market Street just north of the public square. She was about fourteen years younger than her husband. Her remains now rest in Washington Street cemetery, Williamsport, in the family lot of her son.

James Hepburn and his wife Mary had issue :

6.   *i. Samuel*, b. November 5, 1782; m. Ann Clay; d. October 16, 1865, in Lock Haven.

7.   *ii. Andrew D.*, b. May 23, 1786; m. Martha Huston; d. March 6, 1861, in Williamsport.

    iii. William, b. May 23, 1786; d. September 22, 1800.

8.   *iv. James*, b. May 19, 1789; m. Maria Hyatt; d. December 25, 1855, in Philadelphia.

    v. John, b. October 8, 1792. Settled at Northumberland. Served as an ensign in Capt. William F. Buyers' company of Northumberland Blues, attached to the regiment of Lt. Col. George Weirick, 1st Brigade, 2d Division, commanded by Gen. Henry Spearing, war of 1812. Married Juliana, daughter of Col. Thomas and Deborah (nee Martin) Grant, of Sunbury, and d. January, 1838, at Columbia, Pa., and was there buried. His wife, b. May 13, 1798; d. March 8, 1844, at Philadelphia, and was buried by his side in the Presbyterian Churchyard, Columbia. No issue.

9.   *vi. Jane*, b. March 19, 1795; m. Francis C. Campbell; d. May 17, 1867, in Williamsport.

10. *vii. Mary*, b. May 6, 1797; m. James Merrill; d. June 3, 1825, in New Berlin.

11. *viii. Hopewell*, b. October 28, 1799; m. Caroline Cauffman; d. February 4, 1863, in Philadelphia.

12. *ix. Sarah*, b. September 10, 1801; m. James Armstrong; d. February 20, 1829, in Williamsport.

JUDGE WILLIAM HEPBURN AND FAMILY.

III. WILLIAM HEPBURN,[2] (Samuel,[1]) brother of James, was born in County Donegal, Ireland, in 1753, and died at Williamsport, Pa., June 25, 1821. He accompanied his brother to America in 1773, and soon after landing made his way to the West Branch Valley of the Susquehanna, where he located and spent the balance of his days. Throughout his life he was closely associated with his brother, and as has been shown, was identified with him in some of his most extensive land operations. He early showed an active and enterprising disposition, and soon became prominent among the pioneers who had preceded him to the rich and beautiful valley where he took up his abode. Whether he had any acquaintances here at the time of his arrival is unknown, but it is probable that he had. Andrew Culbertson, also a native of Ireland, born not far from the birthplace of Hepburn, had preceded him to this country, and purchasing a large body of land, had settled on what is now the site of the borough of DuBoistown, on the south bank of the river, opposite what is now the western part of the city of Williamsport. Culbertson, who was more than twenty years the senior of Hepburn, at once saw the necessity of building a mill to supply the settlers with flour. The point

JUDGE WILLIAM HEPBURN.

he selected for his permanent residence was at the mouth of a strong stream of water which dashed through a gap in Bald Eagle Mountain and afforded sufficient power to drive his mill. When he commenced building his mill we find young Hepburn in his employ, engaged with others in digging the race to convey the water which was to drive the wheels. This is the first recorded account we have of his work, and the old mill race remains to this day as a reminder of the beginning of the humble labors of a young man who in time reached the distinguished and honorable positions of State Senator and President Judge.

Soon after Culbertson commenced his improvements, the Indians became troublesome, and by their hostile demonstrations kept the settlers in a constant state of alarm. Young Hepburn quickly manifested the characteristic traits of his Scotch-Irish ancestors, and laying down his spade responded to the call for assistance. We soon find him a member of the county militia enrolled for the defense of the frontier, and from that time to the close of the Revolutionary war he was closely identified with the local military arm, and was a participant in many of the bloody and thrilling scenes which occurred in the fair valley where he had resolved to make his home.

IN THE MILITARY SERVICE.

In 1778 he had command of a company of militia, with headquarters at Fort Muncy, ten miles east of Williamsport, and was constantly on the alert to avoid being surprised by the savages who infested the country and were bent on killing and scalping men, women and children, and destroying their cabins and improvements. On the 10th of June of this year occurred a bloody massacre* in what is now almost the central part of the city of Williamsport, when

---

* For a full account of this bloody affair see Hist. Lycoming County, pp. 122-126; also Hist. West Branch Valley, pp. 494-502.

several men, women and children were cruelly butchered, and two little girls carried captives to Canada. On the alarm being given, Captain Hepburn quickly came from the fort with a body of men, cared for the wounded, and buried the mangled dead. The scene presented to Hepburn and his party was one of the saddest witnessed in the valley during the war. The dead were buried near where they fell, and their place of interment became a cemetery, which was used for fully three-quarters of a century, or until the advancing wave of civilization demanded the ground for other purposes. And, as a part of this sad incident, it may be related that forty-three years afterwards the remains of the brave Captain Hepburn were laid in the same grave-yard.

STIRRING EVENTS.

Swiftly on the heels of this massacre followed the great event in the pioneer history of this valley known as the "Big Runaway." Col. Samuel Hunter, who had command of Fort Augusta, forty miles down the river, being apprised by spies and scouts of the approach from the north of a strong body of savages, issued an order to Captain Hepburn to notify the inhabitants to fly at once to Fort Augusta if they would save their lives. The order was promulgated and a panic and flight were the result, the exciting scenes of which beggar description.

On the 10th of June, 1778, Captain Hepburn united with 142 of the residents of the valley north and west of Muncy Hills in an appeal to the Supreme Executive Council, sitting at Philadelphia, for aid and protection. They set forth in strong language the necessity for more troops, and showed their inability to guard a frontier of forty miles with 73 men, the total number of the available force. Referring to the bloody events of that day the petitioners continued: "The very alarming event of the murder and captivity of thirteen of our near neighbors and most intimate acquaintances this day has driven the majority of us to desperation, and to pray that you in your wisdom will order to our immediate relief such standing forces as will be equal to our necessity."

But this appeal came too late. The enemy was already moving. The affair on the Loyalsock, where Peter Wyckoff was captured, and the massacre at Wyoming, caused Colonel Hunter to issue his order to abandon the country. The flight commenced in July, 1778, and in a few days the valley was depopulated, save what militia remained with Hepburn to protect the rear. The families of the settlers were sent down the river on rafts, canoes, flatboats, and whatever crafts could be improvised to transport them and their household goods, whilst cattle and horses were driven by the men on land. Whilst serving with the militia Hepburn had an opportunity to thoroughly acquaint himself with the topography of the country, and note where the finest lands were located. He made his headquarters about the mouth of Loyalsock with the Covenhovens, and other families, and at Fort Muncy, which he commanded at the time of the flight. It has been shown that his brother James frequently visited the valley and kept in close communication with him during the exciting times of Indian trouble. It will be remembered that before the Indians had become aggressive he had entered into an article of agreement with Peter Wyckoff to purchase 600 acres of land on the Loyalsock, in which his brother James was jointly interested. The history of this transaction and the magnificent results which flowed from it, have been minutely described.

FIRST MARRIAGE.

Before these great troubles came upon the country— sometime in 1777—William Hepburn married Crecy Covenhoven. Her family came from New Jersey and settled near the mouth of Loyalsock Creek, probably as early as 1771.

Other settlers in this neighborhood—notably the Wyckoffs
—were from New Jersey also.   In fact there was a colony of
New Jersey people here at that time.   Crecy was a sister of
Robert Covenhoven, the celebrated Indian scout and Revolutionary soldier, who rendered such signal service in the
cause of liberty during the exciting times on the West Branch
of the Susquehanna.   When the "Big Runaway" was precipitated William Hepburn had been married about a year,
as their first child was born August 22, 1778, about two
months after the flight.   Where this event occurred is unknown.   It might have been at Northumberland, where
many of the fugitives from the valley tarried—or possibly
at Philadelphia.   She returned with her husband, became
the mother of ten children, and died April 8, 1800, at their
log house on the Deer Park farm, at the age of 41 years.

As soon as it was safe Hepburn and family were among
the first to return to the Loyalsock.   This was as early as
1779 or 1780.   Before the close of the war he settled on
Deer Park tract and built a log house and out-buildings.
There he lived to the close of his life, and there he raised
his large family, as well as several grandchildren.

JUSTICE, MERCHANT AND FARMER.

The first civil office we find him invested with, after the
return of peace, was that of Overseer of Loyalsock Township
in 1787.   Two years subsequently he received two com-
missions, dated July 2, 1789, signed by Thomas Mifflin,
President of the Supreme Executive Council under the
Constitution of 1776.   Each commission authorized a service of seven years ; one empowered him to transact business
which would go before the Court of Common Pleas, and the
other before the Orphans' Court.   This township had been
created by a decree of the Court of Northumberland County
at February sessions, 1786, and within its boundaries Williamsport was afterwards laid out.   The Constitution of 1790

having effected radical changes in the civil administration of affairs, by wiping out all previous appointments, Thomas Mifflin, who succeeded to the office of Governor, straightway re-appointed Mr. Hepburn Justice of the Peace under date of September 1, 1791, and the limitation was confined to the period in which he should "behave himself well!" His district now comprised the townships of Loyalsock, Lycoming and Pine, a territory greater than some of the counties of to-day.

As population increased there was a demand for a store, where goods and supplies could be obtained without going a long distance. This induced Hepburn to start such an establishment about 1790, and he became the *first* merchant in the settlement which ultimately developed into the city of Williamsport. The mercantile firm of Hepburn & Cowden was then in successful operation at Northumberland, and it is probable that William had the advice and assistance of his brother James in starting this new enterprise. Owing to the difficulty of marketing their grain at that time many farmers started distilleries, because whiskey was a more merchantable and profitable commodity. Culbertson had one near his mill on the opposite side of the river. This induced Hepburn to start one also. And early in the last decade of the eighteenth century he found himself engaged in farming, distilling, merchandising, and conducting the office of a Justice of the Peace. At that time he was the only justice for miles around and much business came before him. He was noted for his wit, quickness of repartee and kindness of heart. Among the anecdotes that have been preserved two may be mentioned. One day he was waited on by a young man named John Bennett, who had paddled his sweetheart in a canoe down the river five or six miles for the purpose of having the marriage ceremony performed. The 'Squire promptly united them, when the groom hesitatingly informed him that he did not have enough money to pay the fee and buy a few articles necessary for housekeeping. The 'Squire was so impressed with the frankness and honest appearance of Mr. Bennett that he not only remitted the fee, but supplied him with some provisions from his store, and sent the newly married couple up the river rejoicing in their canoe.

On another occasion an Irishman named Conn had a suit before him, and taking exceptions to some of his rulings, gave vent to his feelings in personal abuse of the justice. Instead of commanding him to be silent, or imposing a fine, the "'Squire" quickly threw off all dignity, and walking from behind his desk, with one blow of his fist sent Conn sprawling on the floor. No further interruption occurred during the progress of the trial, but the defendant never forgot the blow, and attempted to waylay the "'Squire" after he became Judge, but his strong arm did not fail him, and Conn, again discomfited, concluded not to interfere further with the muscular representative of justice.

After having carried on his store alone for several years he took in S. E. Grier as a partner, and they were associated in business for several years. Grier was made the first postmaster of Williamsport, August 12, 1799, and served until April 20, 1819. Hepburn had much business with Michael Ross, who was the founder of the town.

AS A LAND OWNER.

William did not seem to have been imbued with such a desire to acquire land as his brother James. The first purchase on his individual account, of which we have any record, was at a sheriff's sale in 1789. Flavel Roan, sheriff of Northumberland County, sold a tract of 300 acres belonging to Edmund Huff, on a judgment for debt for £226, and Hepburn became the purchaser and received a deed from the sheriff. This tract laid on the west side of Lycoming Creek and adjoined lands of "John Sutton and Mary Kempleton."

On the 14th of September, 1791, he purchased a "moiety and half" of 200 acres from Richard Parker, of Cumberland County, in consideration of £12, "lawful money of Pennsylvania." This tract was situated in Loyalsock Township and adjoined lands of the Widow Duncan and George North— probably near the present northern boundaries of the city of Williamsport.

By warrant dated June 8, 1792, he acquired a tract of land called "Williamsburg," which contained 315 acres. December 1, 1795, he sold 157 acres and 147 perches off the tract to Alexander Smith for $473.21. There were some improvements on it.

May 4, 1796, he purchased four lots of Michael Ross, in the town of Williamsport, which had just been laid out, in consideration of £182 10s. Two of these lots (25 and 26) were situated on Front Street; the other two (186 and 187) were on the north-east side of the public square. These purchases were made at the time when a great strife was going on for the selection of Williamsport as the county seat.

On the 8th of February, 1797, he purchased from John Sutton lots 43 and 44, being part of his tract called New Garden,—afterwards known as Newberry,—containing three acres. The price paid was £30.

Under date of April 6, 1797, John Maffet sold him, in consideration of $1,000, a tract of land in Lycoming Township called "Corn Bottom," containing 316 acres. The next purchase was a tract of 66¾ acres at sheriff's sale, for £324, lying in the vicinity of Corn Bottom, about two miles up the stream known as "Quinashahaque." This deed is dated June 2, 1801. Previous to this, however, he purchased 90 acres for £130, which was sold by the sheriff as the property of Matthew Wilson, his son-in-law. It was situated in Lycoming Township, on Pine Run. The sale was on a judgment obtained by Meeker & Cochran, merchants of Philadelphia, who sold goods to Wilson, who had started a store. The sale was made October 4, 1800. September 24, 1800, he purchased of James Grier, for £46 12s., six acres and 35 perches lying on the public road west of Newberry.

The next purchase of any importance was made May 22, 1813, when, in connection with his son-in-law, Robert Mc-Clure, he bought the John Edminston tract of 223 acres of his executors for $400. It was situated on Dougherty's Run, about two miles from its mouth.

His last purchase was a tract of 294 acres of Thomas Holliday, September 6, 1814, for $1,737. This was known as the Duncan estate and laid in Loyalsock Township. The last transaction in which he appears in the record books as a grantee is in the deed of partition with his brother James, when they divided the Deer Park and Mount Joy tracts, now embraced in the centre of Williamsport. Deer Park, on which he had lived for over thirty years, contained 316 acres and was a splendid property. The deed of partition may be seen in Book T, p. 402, Williamsport.

From the foregoing statement of his purchases it will be seen that he owned altogether during his lifetime nearly 1,500 acres, besides five or six town lots. The reader will understand that he did not own this quantity all at one time, as he frequently made sales. His Deer Park farm and a few other tracts were all that he possessed at the time of his death, which will be shown by his will.

STATE SENATOR AND JUDGE.

As early as 1786 the agitation for a division of Northumberland County commenced, and was prosecuted vigorously for nine years before the object was accomplished. The county at that time extended to the Allegheny River and the New York State line, covering a vast extent of country, much of which was a primitive wilderness. The project for division met with violent opposition from Robert Morris and other large land owners, who feared that a dismemberment of the county would militate against their interests. Morris, who was known as the "financier of the Revolution," owned thousands of acres of land in Northumberland County, besides tens of thousands in New York State, in what was afterwards known as the Phelps & Gorham purchase, embracing the Genesee country. His lands in Northumberland were largely in that portion which afterwards fell to Lycoming when a division was effected.

Many petitions were laid before the Legislature praying for a division of the great county of Northumberland during the nine years that the struggle continued, but a secret influence always succeeded in upsetting the prayers of the petitioners. The Senatorial district in 1794 was composed of the counties of Luzerne, Mifflin and Northumberland, and William Montgomery was Senator. He resigned before the close of his term, and at a special election held January 8, 1794, William Hepburn was elected to fill the vacancy by a majority of 64 over Rosewell Wells. This was a great triumph for the friends of division. Hepburn was active, untiring and vigilant in his efforts for the erection of a new county, and his persistency soon made a favorable impression. Finally, in conference committees of the two houses, the bill was agreed to April 13, 1795, and immediately signed by Governor Mifflin. The credit for securing the final passage of the bill belonged largely to the persistent and determined efforts of Senator Hepburn, and as a recognition of his services and abilities the Governor appointed him chief of four associate judges April 15, 1795, for the purpose of organizing the judicial machinery of the new county. In a few days the associates met and organized by electing Senator Hepburn president, and he thus became the *first* President Judge of the new county of Lycoming. On the 20th of April he resigned the office of

State Senator and immediately entered on the discharge of his judicial duties.

The selection of a site for the county seat was the next exciting question which arose. The Hepburn brothers were constantly on the alert to advance their interests as landed proprietors. Michael Ross owned about 300 acres of land which adjoined the Mount Joy tract (owned by James Hepburn) on the east. The tradition is that the Hepburns urged Ross to lay out a town on his land and contend for its selection as the county seat. Whether the tradition is true or not is unknown, but subsequent events justify the conclusion that there was foundation for it. Ross quickly acted on the suggestion, laid out his town in 1795, set apart lots for the public buildings, and called it Williamsport. When the commissioners came to locate the site a bitter fight ensued with rivals for location, but after a severe struggle Williamsport was chosen and the court house and jail were erected on lots which Michael Ross donated for that purpose. The fact that the land on which the original part of the town was built was not as good as that owned by the Hepburns, shows that they calculated that in time the town would advance westward and occupy their land. This view of the future was realized. The land comprising their magnificent estate has long since been built over and now forms the central part of the city. The street bounding the Mount Joy tract on the east was named Hepburn, and it still remains to perpetuate the names of the sagacious and far-seeing brothers.

Although William Hepburn was a man without legal learning, he discharged the duties of judge with ability and fairness; he was endowed with a large amount of what is termed "hard common sense," which, combined with a clear, decisive, executive mind, enabled him to succeed where others would have failed. His intellectual faculties being above mediocrity, association and experience enabled him to advance rapidly in his judicial capacity, and ere the close of his term of office, which lasted for ten years, he came to be regarded as a good common pleas judge. Of course, there was a judge learned in the law who presided over the large judicial district, who sat at intervals to hear important causes involving difficult questions of law, but in minor questions Hepburn and his associates were able to hear and decide all matters coming before them.

Judge Hepburn was a Covenanter and remained true to the faith of his fathers. As early as 1786 there was a society of Presbyterians in his settlement, and he was active in promoting the cause of religion. When the Rev. Isaac Grier was sent as missionary to the West Branch in 1792 by the Presbytery of Carlisle, he arrived on the 22d of June of that year at the house of Hepburn, and on the 24th he preached there. Among the early records of the Lycoming Presbyterian Church the name of Judge Hepburn frequently appears as a contributor to its support. He also served as treasurer. The late Tunison Coryell, in his historical reminiscences, thus speaks of him:

The Judge was one of the supporters of the first Presbyterian Church built at Newberry. A receipt of the Rev. Isaac Grier, the pastor, to William Hepburn, dated February 20, 1796, as treasurer of Lycoming Congregation, for "£5 19s. 3½d., full amount of the first year's salary due from said congregation, the 3d of October, 1794," has been preserved.

From an old record it appears that the Judge had large money transactions with Philadelphians and others in 1792. A receipt before us is shown that Thomas McClintock in 1796 was paid £30 in full for one year's work. Also one other receipt, dated July 11, 1796, for £100 in specie in full for a negro boy named Oliver, sold by William Gray, Esq., of Sunbury. October 20, 1798, he paid Thomas Hamilton $30 on account of excise, and about the same date $6.31 is paid Matthew Wilson [his son-in-law], collector of United States revenue, direct tax for property in Loyalsock Township.

The Judge built the present brick building and kitchen on the Deer Park farm in 1801. Jacob Hyman was the carpenter, and he was paid £217 7s. 1od. in full, including the painting, for the work.

He was fond of company and entertained his friends and acquaintances with the greatest hospitality; he had a noble heart and a strong mind, which was well cultivated for a gentleman without opportunities of a good education, was kind and benevolent, and had hosts of warm friends. He was generally correct in his conclusions upon the bench, and was considered one of the leading associates.

HIS ASSESSMENTS.

The first assessment of the taxable inhabitants of Loyalsock Township, made February, 1796, the first year after the erection of Lycoming County, shows William Hepburn to have been possessed of the following property: "Sixty acres cleared and one still house, £225; 300 acres, 2 log houses, 1 log barn, £90; 5 cows, £15; 3 horses, £18; one store, £50; one log cabin and 5 cattle, £18." One hundred and fifty acres unseated land on Lycoming Creek was rated at 15s. per acre. In 1802, six years later, he was assessed with "124 acres cleared land, valued at $3.50 per acre; one *brick* house, $100; one barn, $50; one still house, $200; four horses, $16; eight cows, $5; occupation as judge and storekeeper, $230." His total taxable property was valued at $1,093.60.

In 1821, the year he died, he was assessed as follows:

200 acres, valued at $ 6, ...	$1,200
40 " " " 18, ...	720
60 " " " 12, ...	720
1 House, ...	500
1 Distillery, ...	500
4 Horses and six Cattle, ...	128
6 Houses, ...	50
Occupation, ...	100
Total valuation, ...	$3,918

The tax on this assessment was $19.59. The previous year it was $14.59.

Between the years 1801 and 1802 he erected the brick
dwelling house near where his log houses stood. The
exact time is shown by the assessments, as the brick house
first appears in the list for 1802. This house, which was
considered a very fine one for the time, was built of brick
manufactured on the premises. It stands to-day as a landmark, surrounded by board piles, and is correctly shown in
the illustration. Here in the closing years of his life he dis-
pensed an elegant hospitality, as he was very fond of company, and men of note were frequent guests at his home.

JUDGE HEPBURN'S RESIDENCE, BUILT IN 1801.

In 1804 Loyalsock Township was divided by the erection of Hepburn, and so named in honor of Judge Hepburn.
It has lost much of its territory during the last ninety years,
but still retains its original name.

To Judge Hepburn belongs the credit of being the first
officer of Lodge No. 106, F. & A. M., Williamsport, which
was constituted July 1, 1806, by special dispensation di-

rected to John Cowden, John Boyd, James Davidson and Enoch Smith, past masters. On that date they met and installed William Hepburn, W. M.; James Davidson, S. W.; Samuel Coleman, J. W., and John Kidd, Secretary. A strong anti-Masonic sentiment prevailed at that time, and it required considerable nerve to hold such an office in the face of public opinion, but Hepburn was equal to the emergency. He was re-elected for 1807, 1811 and 1815.

AS A PATRIOT.

That Judge Hepburn was an exceedingly patriotic man is not strange, when we remember the trying times he passed through in fighting against a savage foe, hired by the British to commit the most atrocious deeds of blood against the early settlers. An account of a Fourth of July celebration in 1806, printed in the local paper of Williamsport at that time, reads:

To celebrate the anniversary of the glorious period which gave birth to the freedom and independence of our country, a respectable number of gentlemen of this [Williamsport] borough assembled on Monday on the bank of the Susquehanna. William Hepburn, Esq., was chosen president, and Mr. Charles Stewart vice-president. After partaking of a collation twenty-three toasts were drank.

[A few culled from the list will show the spirit which animated the meeting.]

George Washington—As a hero and statesman, the pride of America, and the admiration of the world—nine cheers and a volley.

Our country—Proud of its national honor, may it never cringe to a foreign power—five cheers and a volley.

Hemp—May there be a sufficiency of it for all who barter the liberties of their country—three cheers and a volley.

The Susquehanna—So long as liberty is dear, may its banks give us an annual repast—six cheers and a volley.

Voluntary by Judge Hepburn—All friends to our coun-

try—May they never want spirit nor courage to defend it—
three cheers and a volley.

By Mr. Coleman*—Napoleon—May storms, hurricanes,
thunder and lightning conspire together to sink him to the
ocean's bottom, if he ever attempts to leave the European
continent with his armies—six cheers and a volley.

The next honor conferred upon him was a commission
from Gov. Thomas McKean, under date of June 4, 1807,
appointing him Major General of the Tenth Division of
the State militia, composed of the counties of Lycoming,
Tioga, Potter, Jefferson, McKean and Clearfield, to serve
four years from the 3d of August following. He filled the
appointment to the satisfaction of the Governor and retired
clothed with military honors in 1811.

He was now nearly sixty years of age, but still retained
a healthy, vigorous constitution, and took an active part in
the management of his store and farm. Some years afterwards, in order to relieve himself from the pressure of business cares, he associated his son Samuel with him in the
store, who, although quite young, aided him greatly.

Matters ran along smoothly for ten years, when the vet-
eran soldier, judge, merchant, and farmer, began to show
signs of rapid decline, and falling violently ill in June,
1821, he died on the 25th of that month, aged 68 years, in
his brick mansion at the foot of Park Street. He was buried
in the old graveyard on West Fourth Street, where he had
assisted in burying those who were so mercilessly slain
by the savages on the 10th of June, 1778. In this grave-
yard† he had reserved for himself and family a plot of

---

*Dr. Samuel Coleman, the second resident physician of Williamsport,
was a Scotchman and no friend of Bonaparte. He afterwards moved to
Clearfield County, named the Grampian Hills, and died there in 1819.

†The ground for this graveyard, comprising one acre and a quarter, was
conveyed to the "Lycoming Congregation," (Deed Book V, p. 385,) by
Amariah Sutton, March 20, 1776, in consideration of five shillings. In a deed
of release to Amariah Sutton, et al., trustees, by Joseph Williams and his wife

ground 33 x 28 feet. Here he rested with his two wives until 1888, when preparations to build a church on the sacred spot necessitated the removal of the remains of himself, wife and several relatives, to Wildwood.

HIS WILL.

The will of Judge Hepburn, evidently drawn by his own hand, gives the reader an insight of the character and traits of the man. It is longer than such documents usually are, but when the extent of his family is considered surprise ceases. It may be found in Will Book I, p. 136, and is as follows:

This is the last will and testament of me the undersigned William Hepburn, Associate Judge of the Court of Common Pleas of Lycoming County:

First. I direct my executors to pay all of my just debts and—

Secondly. It is my will, and I do so order, that my Mansion farm remain, after my decease, in the occupancy and possession of my wife and family until the same shall be sold by my executors, as is hereinafter provided, for the special purpose of aiding in the maintenance and support of my wife (if she shall remain my widow) and such of my children as shall be unmarried at the time of my decease, and shall live with me at that time on the said farm, and shall thereafter continue to live thereon. And it is my further will, and I do so order and direct, that until the said farm be sold, as aforesaid, my said wife (provided she continues my widow as aforesaid) and family shall, with the said farm, have the use and enjoyment of all such implements of husbandry, stock, household furniture and personal property of any description, in the house and on the said farm,

Letitia, heirs of Sutton, (Deed Book VI, p. 135,) made August 7, 1804, occurs this clause: "It is also agreed at said time between said parties that William Hepburn, Esq., is to have a privilege and property in the contents of thirty-three feet long and twenty-eight wide, and part now occupied by him, the said William Hepburn, within the above described premises." The original deed stipulated that it was to be used as a "burial ground forever."

as my executors, in their discretion, shall deem necessary to the proper management thereof, and the comfort and accommodation of my said family.

My stills and all other vessels and utensils belonging to the distillery, together with all other such personal property I may die possessed of, as may not, in the discretion of my executors, be needed in my family as aforesaid, I do hereby order and direct my executors to sell and dispose of as soon after my decease as conveniently may be, and all the residue of my personal property left with my family on the Mansion farm as above said, I do also hereby direct my executors to sell and dispose of as soon after the sale of the Mansion farm as may be.

Thirdly. It is my will and I do hereby empower my executors, or a majority of them, to sell and convey in fee simple, the whole of my real estate, wheresoever the same may be situated, at such time, in such manner, and upon such conditions as they, or a majority of them, shall think right.

Fourthly. The proceeds of my personal estate, if any after the payment of my just debts and funeral expenses, shall be added to the proceeds of my real estate, and the whole together shall form one aggregate fund to be divided and disposed of as follows: That is to say, it shall be divided into as many shares as I have children now living, together with two more shares for my wife Betsey and the children of my late daughter Eliza. Each of my children now living shall receive one share; my dear wife Betsey one share and a half, and the two children of my late daughter Eliza half a share. To my wife and to such of my children as are of age, or are married, their respective shares shall be paid as the proceeds of my estate are received; but the shares of such of my children as are minors shall be put out to interest in some public funds, or bank stock, or on real security, or otherwise, as my executors may deem most for the benefit of my said children, and the interest thereof applied to their support until they shall arrive at full age or marry, unless my executors should deem it necessary to apply a part of the principal also to this purpose, which they may do at any time if they find the interest too small a sum for the support of the minor child.

With regard to the half share bequeathed to the children of my late daughter Eliza, it is my will that the same disposition be made of it by my executors as is above provided in the case of my own minor children. It is further my will, with regard to the said half share, that if either of the children of my said late daughter Eliza die before my decease, or in its minority, the survivor shall have the full half share aforesaid; and if both of the said children die in their minority and without issue, that the said half share shall sink into my estate and be divided as I have heretofore directed amongst my children.

With regard to the children of my late daughter Janet Wilson, I consider the large advances made to their parents, in their lifetime, and the expenses incurred since their decease and yet to be incurred in maintaining and educating their children, as fully equivalent to the interest of any one of my children in my estate. With these considerations I bequeath them (the surviving children of my late daughter Janet Wilson) a certain tract of land called Fairfield, patented in the name of Janet Wilson the 17th of April, 1794, but all expenses paid by me and all receipts in my name; and lest any doubts should arise with my heirs as to her title being sufficient, I do now bequeath said tract of land to her children, which land is situated on the waters of Hammond's Run, in Northumberland (now Lycoming) County beginning at a post, thence by land of William Winter, south thirty-three degrees west two hundred and ninety-two perches to a post, thence by vacant land north eighty-four degrees east seventy-three perches to an ash, north eighteen degrees east one hundred and five perches to a white oak, north-east one hundred and eighteen perches to a white oak, north ten degrees west thirty-four perches to a pine, north seventy-three degrees west one hundred and fifty perches to a black oak, south forty-six perches to a hickory and north seventy-nine degrees west one hundred and thirty perches to the beginning, containing 216 acres, three perches and an allowance of six per cent. for roads, &c. I do also bequeath unto Mary Wilson, Samuel Wilson, Matilda Wilson and Robert Wilson, children of my late daughter Janet Wilson, the sum of $200 each, to be paid when my executors think most expedient.

Fifthly. If any of my children now alive should marry and die leaving issue between the time of making and executing the present will and my own death, such issue shall be entitled in equal proportion to the share that would otherwise have belonged to the parent, to be invested by my executors, for his or their use, in some safe or proper security, to be paid to such, my grandchild or grandchildren, when he or they shall attain the age of twenty-one, or marry, except so much thereof as may be necessary for the support and education of such grandchild or children, to which the interest shall always first be applied.

Sixthly. Should any of my children die after my decease in their minority and without issue, the share, or what remains thereof, to such child so dying, shall be divided amongst the rest of my children, or their issue, respectively, on the principle aforesaid.

Seventhly. Whereas one-third part of my personal property, and one-third of the annual proceeds of my real property, would amount, as I conceive, to a share out of proportion, and far greater than my wife is reasonably entitled to, considering my numerous family, my will is that the share and half share before mentioned and bequeathed to my present wife shall be considered in lieu and bar of all dower and claim of dower to which she may be entitled; and if after my decease she should think proper to reject the provision herein made for her, and lay claim to her legal dower out of my estate, then my will is that the said share and half share bequeathed to her, together with all the shares herein bequeathed to my children by her shall be null and void, and the same shall go to increase the aggregate, and to be divided among my other children by my former wife, and I leave the children by my present wife Betsey to be supported by her alone out of such her dowry, conscientiously believing that the disposition in this present will made is fair and equitable between my children and my present wife.

Eighthly. Whereas a partnership now exists between my son Samuel and myself in a store in Williamsport, in which I have advanced $4,000 as permanent stock, which $4,000 is to be refunded at my decease, out of the funds of the

store, if not done before. The house and two lots now occupied by my son Samuel in Williamsport I do value at
$4,000, and it being my desire that the business of said
store shall proceed without interruption or embarrassment
after my decease, it is therefore my will, and I do hereby
direct, if my said son Samuel shall agree thereto, and consent under such arrangement to continue the same store upon
his own account, and take the house and lots at the price I
have put upon them, that the sum of $2,000, part of the said
$4,000, shall bear interest for one year after my decease,
and that my said son shall pay to my executors yearly
after my decease the sum of $800 until the said sum of
$4,000 and the interest as aforesaid, shall be fully paid and
discharged; and when so paid and discharged, and my
interest in the profits of the said store (as per the written
article between my said son and myself) is arranged to the
satisfaction of my executors, the said store buildings and
lots shall be the sole and absolute property and estate of my
said son Samuel. The money to be received from my said
son as aforesaid to constitute a part of the aggregate of my
estate after payment of debts, and to be divided amongst
my children as aforesaid.

Ninthly. I constitute and appoint Robert McClure, Esq.,
and my sons Samuel Hepburn, William Hepburn, and
James Hepburn, to be executors of this will, and guardians
of such of my children as may be minors at the time of my
decease—of such my executors, or a majority, may act, and
if any one should die, a majority of the survivors may appoint another guardian in his place, if deemed necessary.
I also appoint Alexander Stewart as one of the guardians
for my minor children.

[Signed]   WILLIAM HEPBURN.

Signed, sealed and delivered in the presence of us,
this 25th day of June, 1821.

JOHN CUMMINGS,
JAMES McCLINTOCK.

The will was probated June 28, 1821, before Joseph
Foulke, Register and Recorder.

As before stated, Judge Hepburn married, first, Crecy
Covenhoven [b. N. J., 1759,] in 1777, and they had issue:

13.   *i. Janet,* b. August 22, 1778; m. Matthew Wilson; d. July 6, 1811.
14.   *ii. Mary,* b. 1780; m. Robert McClure; d. December 17, 1839.
       iii. Elizabeth, b. 1782; m. Alexander Stewart; d. March 29, 1817;
             left two sons, Charles and William Stewart.
       iv. Matilda, b. October 3, 1784; m. Alexander Stewart, widowed
             husband of her sister Elizabeth; d. October 30, 1866; no issue.
       v. Lucy, b. 1786; d. January, 1864, unmarried.
15.   *vi. Sarah,* b. 1788; m. Col. Alexander Cummings of the U. S. A.
       vii. Mercy, b. 1790; m. Dr. William R. Power; both d. in Phila-
             delphia; time unknown; no issue.
       viii. William, b. 1792; was one of the executors of his father's estate;
             evidently d. before 1831, as in that year James, the sole surviv-
             ing executor, sold the mansion house property; was unmarried.
       ix. Samuel, b. 1795; m. Sarah Cowden; d. August 22, 1824. Was
             interested with his father in a store, and owned lots No. 186 and
             187, Williamsport. His estate, on appraisement, footed up as
             follows: Brick house, $3,050; store and lots, $680.35. His
             widow subsequently m. James Merrill, Esq., of New Berlin.
16.   *x. James,* b. April 14, 1799; m., first, Rebecca Cowden; second,
             Julia Baldwin, of Elmira.

Mrs. Crecy Covenhoven Hepburn having died April 8,
1800, Judge Hepburn married, secondly, Elizabeth, daughter
of Thomas and Jane Walker Huston, of Williamsport. She
was a sister of Charles Huston, the eminent jurist and Chief
Justice of the Supreme Court of Pennsylvania, and of Martha,
who afterwards married A. D. Hepburn, son of James Hepburn, of Northumberland. Thomas Huston came from
Bucks County, where he had married Jane, daughter of
Charles Walker, (about 1770,) who was a member of the
famous legal family of Ireland, and married Mary McClana-
han, daughter of a Scottish lord. He (Huston) served as a
captain in the Revolutionary war. About the time Williamsport was founded he settled there, and in 1798 built a
log house on the north-west corner of the square, in which
he opened an inn. Several terms of the early courts were

held in one of the rooms of this building. Captain Huston died May 11, 1824, aged 85 years, and his wife followed him July 8, 1824, aged 77 years.

By his second marriage Judge Hepburn had issue:

17. *xi. Crecy*, b. October 1, 1801 ; m. Thomas P. Simmons; d. August 8, 1884, in Williamsport.

18. *xii. Charles*, b. 1802; m. Margaret McMeens; d. at Grand Rapids, Michigan.

19. *xiii. Harriet*, b. November 23, 1804; m. Dr. E. L. Hart, of Elmira; d. August 6, 1892.

20. *xiv. John*, b. November 16, 1806; m. Caroline Wheeler, of Elmira, March 8, 1831; d. November 24, 1878. His wife, b. June 6, 1807, d. August 24, 1878. Both d. in Williamsport.

xv. Cowden, b. September 27, 1808; m. Susan Tuttle; d. March 26, 1877. His wife d. September 13, 1883, aged 73 years, 9 months and 4 days Had three sons and four daughters, viz.: Edward, James, Charles, Frances, Mellicent, Charlotte, and Susan. All are deceased but Frances and Charlotte, and they reside in Kansas.

xvi. Charlotte, b. 1810; m. David Jack, of Boalsburg, Centre County; d. Elmira, 1855. Issue (surname Jack): Elizabeth, Charles, Hepburn, b. April 13, 1840, d. March 19, 1861; Agnes and Crecy. The latter m. Bethel Claxton, of Philadelphia, and d. leaving three sons. Elizabeth, now the only survivor, m. Albert Steele, and lives in Michigan; has one daughter named Charlotte.

xvii. Martha, b. 1812; d. 1817.

21. *xviii. Susan*, b. 1814; m. Rev. G. L. Brown; d. May 5, 1841, leaving an infant daughter.

22. *xix. Huston*, b. August 17, 1817; m., first, Susan McMicken; second, Anna Simmons; d. April 4, 1891.

Mrs. Hepburn, second, born in 1779, d. November 21, 1827, aged 48 years, having survived her husband a few months over six years.

SAMUEL HEPBURN, JR.

IV. SAMUEL HEPBURN,[2] (Samuel,[1]) born in County Donegal, Ireland, in 1755; came to America with his father and brother John. Near the close of the century he settled at Milton, Pa., and opened a store for the sale of merchandise. Milton was laid out in 1792, consequently Samuel Hepburn* was one of the first, if not the *first*, store-keepers in the settlement. He married Edith Miller about 1791, and died December 24, 1801, in the 46th year of his age. His remains were taken to Northumberland and buried by the side of his father, where his tombstone may still be seen.

It appears from the account of his administrators (his brothers James and William), on file at Sunbury, that he was doing a good business for that time, as the inventory foots up over $7,000. On account of many bad debts on his books, considerable time was consumed in settling up his estate, and three different statements were made to the court by the administrators before their account was confirmed and closed.

After his death his widow carried on the store for a few years, when she married, secondly, Samuel Erwin, of Bucks County, and they moved to Painted Post, N. Y., or its vicinity, where he had large landed interests. It is unknown at this writing (July, 1894,) whether there was any issue by the first marriage or not. That there was a family of Erwins at Painted Post is a matter of history; and there is an Erwin Township in Steuben County to-day which took its name from this family.

A SCATTERED FAMILY.

V. JOHN HEPBURN,[2] (Samuel,[1]) born in County Donegal, Ireland, 1757; came to America first with his father and brother Samuel; was sent back in a short time to bring his mother and sister over. The vessel, Faithful Steward, on which they sailed, was lost somewhere on the American coast, and his mother and sister were drowned while trying to get ashore in a small boat, but he was saved and brought the

---

*This Samuel Hepburn must not be confounded with Samuel Hepburn, the eminent lawyer, who settled in Milton about 1801 or 1802, and died at Lock Haven in 1865. The former was an uncle of the latter.

sorrowful tidings to his father and brothers at Northumberland.

That he married Mary Elliott about 1790 is well attested by his descendants now living in Iowa. Her family is supposed to have been living on Chillisquaque Creek, Northumberland County, where many early settlements were made. It is also well attested that they lived in Milton, for their son James, recently deceased, said that he was born there March 2, 1802.

Soon after this the family settled in what is now known as Susquehanna Township, Lycoming County, on a fine level tract of land in the bend of the river, opposite the village of Linden, six miles west of Williamsport. A quit-claim deed, on record at Williamsport, (Book I, p. 22,) made by James, William, John and Edith (Miller) Hepburn, releases (in consideration of $200) to John Miller a lot at Tioga Point, Lycoming County, on which Miller had a storehouse and outbuildings. John Hepburn agreed to take the title to the property at his own risk and pay the consideration. The receipt was attested September 26, 1807, and the deed was executed December 3, 1807. This indicates that the three brothers of Samuel (deceased), and his widow, had some claim on the property. At this time John was about fifty years of age, as he was born in 1757.

John Hepburn * and wife died in "Susquehanna Bottom," but the time cannot be accurately stated. His son James, who died in Iowa in 1885, said that he was about twelve years old when his father died; and as he (James) was born in March, 1802, that would make the time of his death in 1814, at the age of about fifty-eight. The tradition is that he died from the effects of a cancer. His wife died five years later, or in 1819, according to the recollection of her son James.

---

* On a preceding page it was stated that the place where his death occurred was unknown. Since those pages were printed the place has been discovered.

John Hepburn and his wife, Mary Elliott, had issue, all born at Milton :

> i. *Rosana*, b. about 1792; d. 1799.
>
> ii. *Jane*, b. about 1794; d. 1812.
>
> iii. *Isabella*, b. about 1796; m. William Brady and they settled in Woodhull, Steuben County, New York.
>
> iv. *John*, b. about 1798; m. Elizabeth Martin, in what is now Piatt Township, Lycoming County, Pa. She d. early, leaving one son, William G., and two daughters, Sarah and Elizabeth. The son was killed in the first battle of Bull Run. The father d. August, 1859.
>
> v. *Samuel*, b. July 18, 1800; m. Mary Crawford, of Steuben County, New York; d. January 18, 1884, in Level Corner.
>
> vi. *James*, b. March 2, 1802; m. Roxana Simmons; d. February 13, 1885, in Iowa.

James claimed that he had a brother Andrew, but he never knew what became of him. In Bancroft's History of Popular Tribunals, San Francisco, (Vol. 2, p. 47), he mentions an Andrew Hepburn, who appeared as a witness in the trial of Casey, who shot King, a rival editor, in 1856. Perhaps he was the lost brother and a " 49er."

Samuel, the fifth child of the above family, was a resident of Lycoming County about eighty years. When he married Mary Crawford they settled in Level Corner. She was born November 4, 1800, and died August 4, 1880. Soon after the Pennsylvania Canal was opened Samuel secured the appointment of lock-tender at the head of the " nine mile level," and there he remained for twenty-seven years. Owing to his position he made many acquaintances among those who did business on that great water way ; and especially in the days of the packet boats, after the stage coaches were supplanted by this swifter method of transportation, he was known to hundreds of travelers. When the locomotive came his calling was soon ended, and he and his wife retired to live with their son, John C., at whose house they both died at the dates given above.

Samuel Hepburn and his wife, Mary Crawford, had issue:

i. *William*, b. December 23, 1820; m. Margaret Bastian; he died in the army; had one son, Samuel Dale, and two daughters, Henrietta and Martha; his widow and children live in Williamsport.

ii. *Robert*, b. September 7, 1822; m. and lives in Bellefonte; have three sons and one daughter.

iii. *Margaret*, b. December 25, 1824; m. Charles Martin and settled at Canisteo; d. January 17, 1892; her husband died eleven days before her; left three sons.

iv. *Mary P.*, b. December 8, 1826; m. John Gheen; d. November 1, 1885; left three sons and one daughter.

v. *Jane*, b. August 8, 1828; m. Robert Davidson; reside at Jersey Shore; have one son, James.

vi. *Martha*, b. March 30, 1830; m. Warren Clark, of Nippenose Valley; is deceased; no issue.

vii. *Charles*, b. March 4, 1835; m. Rebecca Gillespie; she d. in 1884, leaving four sons and one daughter, viz.: 1. John W., b. September 10, 1866; m. Flora E. Fessler and lives in Williamsport. 2. James D., b. February 21, 1868; m. and lives near Montoursville. 3. Robert W., b. June 9, 1870; single. 4. Wilbur G., b. 1872. 5. Carmina, b. April 9, 1884. Mr. Hepburn lives in Level Corner.

viii. *John C.*, b. November 14, 1837; m. Mary P. Shaffer December 23, 1881; have one son, Walker; live in Linden, Pa.

ix. *Nancy C.*, b. August 8, 1840; m. Warren Clark, widowed husband of her sister Martha; live in Nippenose Valley.

Soon after the death of Mary Elliott Hepburn, mother of John's family, a descendant living in Iowa writes: "The family separated never again to see each other!" James, the youngest of her family of whom we have any record, left home at about the age of eighteen years and made his way to Ontario County, New York, learned the trade of a carpenter, and at Canandaigua, in 1822, married Roxana Simmons. The same year they settled in Olean, New York, where they lived until 1850, when they emigrated to Iowa and located in Polk County—probably near Des Moines, as James was a carpenter and builder. Their children, all born at Olean, were as follows:

i. *John*, b. in 1823; m. and lives at Glencoe, Neb., and has William, Amasa, Charles and Emma. He is a farmer.

ii. *Joseph Addison*, b. April 27, 1827; removed to Iowa March 21, 1850, and to Polk County and Des Moines May 23, 1855; was a merchant; m. Annie E. Jordan January 2, 1866; d. May 3, 1893. Issue: George B., Frank A., Nellie E., and Alice E. Hepburn.

iii. *Mary Elliott*, b. 1829; m. Rev. John A. Nash in 1853, and d. April, 1894. Issue (Surname Nash): 1. John A., Jr., b. May 9, 1854; is a practicing attorney at Audubon, Iowa. 2. Jennie C., m. Rev. C. J. Rose, Oberlin, Ohio. 3. Netta M., m. John McVickar, Des Moines. 4. Harriet M.; single.

iv. *Harriet*, m., 1853, Dr. Joseph A. Davis and lives at Ridgeland, Iowa. Her husband d. August 28, 1884. No Issue.

v. *Maria Elizabeth*, b. 1837; m., 1868, George Dunham.

vi. *Charles S.*, b. 1842; d. of typhoid fever in 1863, while serving in the war of the Rebellion.

Roxana Simmons Hepburn, mother of the above six children, born March 11, 1804, died April 14, 1873, in Des Moines. Her husband survived her about twelve years and died at Ridgeland, Iowa, February 13, 1885, at the ripe age of almost 83 years. When he crossed the plains of Iowa in 1850 with his family, the country was wild and thinly settled, and bands of roving Indians were frequently seen. He lived long enough to see the country reclaimed from its wild state. Near his primitive home the advancing tide of civilization swept grandly by, leaving in its wake populous towns and cities. Yet there is something deeply pathetic in the story that when the members of his father's family parted on the banks of the romantic Susquehanna two generations before his decease, they parted to know each other no more!

A POPULAR MAN AND OFFICER.

On the death of Joseph Addison, second son of James and Mary Elliott Hepburn, the Des Moines *Leader* of May 4, 1893, thus spoke of him:

Every one knew Add. Hepburn. And there is not one in all the county's 80,000 people to take offense at the statement that he had more friends and fewer enemies than any other resident in the city. He had lived a courageous life in Des Moines, and through his manner of bearing misfortunes that would have broken down and killed stronger men, he made every man his friend, his friend indeed.

Mr. Hepburn was the Recorder of Polk County. He was elected by a unanimous vote last November, and was inducted into office the first of January. His extreme popularity insured his nomination by all the political parties, and, the only instance in the history of the county, was elected by receiving every vote cast. Last Thursday he spent the day in his office in the court house, but was suffering from a cold. Nothing serious appeared until Sunday, when physicians were called in and it was discovered that Mr. Hepburn was suffering from an attack of pneumonia developed from the slight cold he had taken the Thursday before. He rapidly grew worse, and yesterday afternoon his strength failed him and he gave up the battle, and his life.

J. Add. Hepburn was born in Olean, N. Y., April 27, 1829, He was therefore 64 years of age. He removed to Iowa, March 21, 1850, and to Polk County and Des Moines May 23, 1855. Here he has lived for nearly forty years. After removing to the city he clerked for James Crane, who maintained a dry goods establishment on Second Street. In 1856, in company with M. A. Woodward, he started a dry goods house, also on Second Street, then the centre of business of the city. Afterwards he was associated with a firm, Morris & Hepburn, and later clerked in Trepanier's establishment.

Five years ago he was compelled to retire from active work and business life because of physical debility. When a small boy he had gone in bathing in very cold water, or had chilled himself in some way, and caught a cold which settled in his right leg, making him lame. He was rejected on that account when he tried to enlist in the army. The limb always troubled him, and about five years ago he was compelled to submit to an amputation of it just below the knee. Soon after another amputation became necessary, and a short time ago another, the last of which left nothing of the member. It was a series of misfortunes and torture that might have broken

the man's spirit and ruined his hope for better things. But
all the people know that Add. Hepburn was made of nobler
stuff. Mr. Hepburn was a Mason and a member of the
Baptist Church. He was one of the old settlers and they
will turn out almost en masse to attend the funeral.

And thus almost in the winking of an eye the life of
Add. Hepburn went out. The noblest epitaph ever spoken of
man has said of him : " He was an honest man." Misfortune filled his life; he endured. Pain racked him; he
smiled. Fortune came ; he greeted her with honesty. He
lived uprightly, he suffered manfully, and died courageously.

HIS WIDOW HONORED BY THE PEOPLE.

Several hours before the spirit of Joseph Addison Hepburn had " passed into the valley of the shadow," two or
three persons had forced themselves upon the Board of Supervisors and importuned them for the appointment to the position death was on the eve of making vacant. They were
repulsed by the board and requested to observe the rules of
propriety and decency in such cases. Such conduct aroused
the indignation of the press, and the *Leader* thus referred
to the matter :

Meantime it is pleasing to know that men, regardless of
party, and moved by chivalrous motives born of generous in-
stincts, so soon as the scramble became known, united in
an almost spontaneous movement to secure the appointment
of Mrs. Hepburn to the place made vacant by the mournful
death of her esteemed and lamented husband. The judges
of the court, scores of attorneys, many of the county offi-
cials, Democrats and Republicans, and in fact almost every-
body concurred in the proposition, and for the purpose of
checkmating the hungry office hunters seeking the place,
delegations were appointed to wait upon such members of
the Board of Supervisors who are in the city, to urge the
appointment of Mrs. Hepburn to the position of Recorder.
This most excellent, but sadly bereaved lady, is said to
possess ample executive ability and business tact to assume
and discharge the duties of the office, and a powerful influence will be exerted to secure her appointment. Every

citizen of Des Moines, who knew Add. Hepburn, and they were legion, will cheerfully extend to his accomplished wife all the assistance possible to persuade the Supervisors to confer upon her the title of the office.

The Board of Supervisors promptly responded to the unanimous demand of public sentiment by appointing Mrs. Hepburn to the position made vacant by the decease of her husband; and, as a further attestation of the popularity of deceased and the esteem and respect entertained for his widow, at the succeeding election she was nominated and elected without opposition! It is doubtful, so far as personal popularity, appreciation and sympathy for two individuals are concerned, if a parallel case can be found in any county of the United States!

A DISTINGUISHED CLERGYMAN.

Mary Elliott Hepburn, their third child and eldest daughter, who became the second wife of Rev. John A. Nash, D. D., a distinguished pioneer Baptist minister, was a lady of culture and refinement, and active in Sunday School and all religious work. Dr. Nash was born in the town of Sherburne, Chenango County, New York, July 11, 1815. The family from which he descended was founded in America in 1649, by Edward Nash, of Stratford, England, who settled near Norwalk, Connecticut. John A. Nash, D. D., died February 14, 1890, under peculiarly painful circumstances, in his 75th year. His death was the result of an accident; while attempting to board a moving train, he was knocked from the platform, sustaining a fracture of the thigh bone, right leg, near the hip. He was taken to his home in Des Moines, where he lay motionless for twelve weeks before he died.

SKETCHES OF THE DESCENDANTS OF JAMES AND WILLIAM HEPBURN.

VI. SAMUEL HEPBURN,[3] (James,[2] Samuel,[1]) born in Philadelphia November 5, 1782; died at Lock Haven October 16, 1865, in the 84th year of his age. He was raised at Northumberland, Pa., and there he received his preparatory education. At a suitable age he entered Princeton College and was graduated therefrom with honor. On his return home he commenced reading law under the direction of the celebrated Jonathan H. Walker, then a resident of his native town, and was admitted to the bar at Sunbury about 1800. He located at Milton, Pa., where his uncles, Samuel and John, were then living, the former engaged in merchandising, and he was the second lawyer to open an office in that place.

At that time Milton was a very small town, but he closely attended to business, and as the place grew his business expanded with it, until he had built up a fine practice. Mr. Hepburn married Miss Ann, daughter of Rev. Slator Clay and Hannah Hughes, widow of John Hughes, of Montgomery County, Pa., about 1811. After living in Milton about forty-five years, they removed to Lock Haven in 1856, in order to be near their two daughters who were residents of that place. There Mr. Hepburn died as stated above. His wife, who was born March 16, 1788, died December 5, 1865, having survived him less than two months.

His character is thus analyzed from a professional and moral standpoint by one who knew him well:

Samuel Hepburn was a lawyer of wide reputation, attend-

ANDREW D. HEPBURN

ing the courts of Northumberland, Lycoming, Montour, Columbia, Union, Centre, and Clinton counties. He was a man of polite and gentlemanly manners, of great integrity and uprightness of character; temperate in his habits, not much given to society, but domestic and retiring, finding his happiness mainly in his own family. He was decided in his political opinions, but no partisan or politician, and not ambitious of place or office. He was a member and elder of the Presbyterian Church, and always took a deep interest in its affairs.

Samuel Hepburn and wife had issue as follows:

23. *i. Hannah Maria*, b. December 25, 1812; m. William H. Blackiston June 8, 1835, and d. June, 1878.

24. *ii. James Curtis*, b. March 13, 1815; m. Clara M. Leete; missionary to China and Japan; now resides in Orange, N. J.

25. *iii. Sarah*, b. June 2, 1817; m. James Pollock December 19, 1837;
d. April 24, 1886.

26. *iv. Slator Clay*, b. October 19, 1819; studied theology and entered
the Presbyterian ministry; stationed at Campbell Hall, N. Y.

27. *v. Mary*, b. May 1, 1822; m. L. A. Mackey; resides in Lock
Haven.

vi. Emma, b. July 22, 1825; m. Hogan Brown.

vii. Louisa Harriet, b. March 7, 1828; m. Edward McClure; resides
in Lock Haven.

viii. Jane, b. December 2, 1830; m. Dr. H. C. Lichtenthaler; d.
August 13, 1872.

VII. ANDREW DOZ HEPBURN,[3] (James,[2] Samuel,[1]) second son of James and Mary Hopewell Hepburn, was born at Northumberland March 10, 1784,* and died at Williamsport March 6, 1861. He was named for Andrew Doz, a resident of Philadelphia, who was appointed "Commissioner of Purchases" for that city by the Supreme Executive Council, April 1, 1780. The letter apprising him of his appointment says: "The very urgent necessity for every exertion in the duties of this office induces the Council to request you will immediately take the qualification required

---

*On page 133 an error occurred in printing the date of his birth. For May 23, 1786, read March 10, 1784.

by law to proceed to purchase—especially forage, for which there is the most pressing necessity, as the public horses are now suffering for want of it." See Vol. VIII., p. 154, Pennsylvania Archives. Doz was an acquaintance of James Hepburn, who was then a merchant in Philadelphia, and such a friendship existed between them that he named his second son after him. He was a descendant of the celebrated Vander Doz, the philosopher, statesman, historian, and defender of Leyden during the siege by the Spaniards. The name has been perpetuated to the present generation by descendants of Andrew Doz Hepburn.

He was educated in the schools of his native town and brought up to the mercantile business in the store of his father. When scarcely eighteen years of age he was sent to Williamsport to look after the landed interests of his father, who owned the Mt. Joy tract of 300 acres, which adjoined the western boundary line of Williamsport, besides other lands in the county of Lycoming. His uncle, Judge William Hepburn, it will be remembered, owned the Deer Park farm, lying west of his father's land.

Soon after his arrival he built a house, opened a store, and became the *second* merchant in Williamsport. It was then a mere hamlet, and a large part of the site of the future city was covered by a forest. The logs for his house were hewn from trees felled from the rear part of the lot, which was situated on the north-west corner of the public square and Market Street. On the 2d of September, 1813, James Hepburn and his wife conveyed (See Deed Book M, p. 67,) this lot and another one (Nos. 183 and 184) to him " in consideration of natural love and one dollar." These lots were originally purchased from Michael Ross. The house was afterwards weather-boarded, and was quite a landmark until it was destroyed by fire several years ago. The site is now occupied by a modern brick block.

In 1802, when less than nineteen years of age, he married Martha, daughter of Thomas and Janet Walker Huston, of Bucks County, mention of whom has been made. She was a sister of Charles Huston, afterwards a justice of the Supreme Court of Pennsylvania, as well as a younger sister of the second wife of his uncle, Judge Hepburn, which also made him the brother-in-law of his uncle. This union proved a long and happy one.

He carried on his mercantile business for several years and was very successful, but after a time he gave himself up to the care of his valuable and increasing property. He purchased and inherited large tracts of land, a portion of which at this time includes a large part of the city. In addition he owned several farms in the vicinity. In 1815 he laid out a number of lots west of Hepburn Street, which he named "Hepburn's Addition." He sold the first sites for saw mills when the lumber industry was beginning to develop, and lived long enough to see it in the full tide of successful operation.

His integrity and standing as a business man is shown by the fact that he was chosen county treasurer in 1806 and served until 1808. He was then only twenty-four years of age. It is rare that this office is conferred upon one so young. He was also identified with the militia at an early date. A book of military tactics, now in the possession of A. D. Hepburn, a grandson, contains this entry in his own handwriting: "Brigade Major, A. D. Hepburn." This rank was equivalent to what is now assistant adjutant general. The time of his military service was somewhere between 1800 and 1810, or perhaps later.

He was studious and industrious. Early in life he made himself familiar with both law and medicine, and always gave these sciences much study and thought. People, therefore, were in the habit, as long as he lived, of going to him for legal advice, and the afflicted often consulted him. He was frequently called on by the court to serve as a commissioner when it was sought to divide a township, sit as an arbitrator, or attend to other business involving good judgment, practical knowledge and experience. In 1824 he was one of three viewers commissioned to divide Lycoming Township; and in 1825 he was called on to serve in the same capacity in the division of Muncy Township. By act of April 14, 1827, he was appointed one of the commissioners to lay out " by courses and distances " a state road from Northumberland to Jersey Shore.

He was quiet and retiring in his manners, possessed an excellent literary taste, with marked intellectual attainments. There were few men in the community more widely known, or whose influence was more generally felt. He was alive to the importance of public improvements, and his pen was ably used in promoting the construction of the West Branch Canal, which he regarded as essential for the development of the country. He was a large shipper of grain down the river by arks to Baltimore, and he saw the necessity of an improved method of transportation by water for the benefit of the business man and farmer.

Mr. Hepburn was a lover of books and a great reader. In the later years of his life he devoted much of his time to the study of theological literature. He was thoroughly conversant with the doctrines of the Presbyterian Church, and it is said of him that ministers of his church were almost afraid to enter his library because of the severe catechising to which he was in the habit of subjecting them. His grandfather, Samuel Hepburn, was prominently connected with the Presbyterian Church of Scotland, and so intense was the religious feeling at that time that he was forced to leave his native land and take refuge in Ireland. His descendants followed in his footsteps in America. The subject of our sketch was one of the first two elders of the church organized in Williamsport, and there has been an uninterrupted line of eldership among his descendants down to the present generation. He also gave a portion of the ground for the first Presbyterian church erected in Williamsport, and very largely bore the expense of the first building, and made provision in his will, under certain conditions, for a building to be used as a parsonage. He also served as superintendent of the Sunday school for many years.

On the 6th of February, 1852, Mr. Hepburn had the misfortune to lose his wife by death. She was born in 1786 and died in the 66th year of her age. They had lived happily together for fifty years, and her demise was a severe blow to him. He survived her for nine years, and died, as stated in the beginning of this sketch, lacking but twenty-six days of being seventy years old. In his will, which is dated August 3, 1860, he carefully divided his large estate among his heirs, and appointed his sons, Andrew and Thomas, executors.

The remains of himself and wife repose in the family lot in the Williamsport Cemetery, Washington Street, where their tombstones may be seen. They left issue:

28.　　*i. James Huston*, b. September 11, 1803; d. July 30, 1853, in Jersey Shore.

　　　ii. Mary, b. September 30, 1805; m. Dr. James Rankin, Muncy; d. January 13, 1853; left two sons, William McGinley and Andrew Hepburn, both deceased, and one daughter, now Mrs. Emily Bear.

29.　　*iii. Samuel*, b. November 26, 1806; living in Carlisle, Pa.

30.　　*iv. Janet*, b. November 29, 1808; living in Muncy.

　　　v. Martha, b. October 28, 1810; m. Dr. Thomas Wood, Muncy; d. July 27, 1846; left one son, Thomas Hopewell Wood, now a resident of Litchfield, Minnesota.

31.　　*vi. William*, b. December, 1812; d. October 5, 1855, in Williamsport.

32.　　*vii. Andrew*, b. December 15, 1814; d. June 10, 1872, in Williamsport.

　　　viii. Charles Walker, b. March 19, 1819; studied law, was admitted to the bar, and d. at Harrisburg September 19, 1842.

　　　ix. Hopewell, b. March 29, 1821; d. July 4, 1844.

33. *x. Thomas*, b.———; d. in Baltimore August 8, 1873.
     xi. Sarah, the youngest daughter, m. Dr. William Hayes and they
          settled in Muncy, Pa.   Issue (surname Hayes) : Ada H., m.
          Mr. Elliot; Mary H., m. Mr. Noble; is deceased.

VIII.   JAMES HEPBURN,[3] (James,[2] Samuel,[1]) fourth son of
James and Mary Hopewell Hepburn, born May 19, 1789,
at Northumberland, Pa.; died December 25, 1855, in Philadelphia.   After receiving a preparatory education in his
native town, he studied law with his brother Samuel, who
had located in Milton, and was admitted to the bar at Sunbury August 19, 1819, and commenced the practice of his
chosen profession.   He at once evinced a talent for business and soon became one of the representative men of the
town.   He was chosen president of the Northumberland
Bank, and bridge company, and was otherwise prominent
in business affairs.   He served as president of the bridge
company from 1830 to 1838.

The bridge across the river to Sunbury was first opened
for travel in 1814, but was not completed until 1818.   His
father had taken a deep interest in the construction of the
bridge, and its opening, a few years before his death, was a
source of much gratification to him, as well as the occasion
for a demonstration in which the people of the town and
surrounding country participated.   The son also was very
much interested in the cause of education.   The Northumberland Academy, a famous institution in its day, and conducted by Rev. Isaac Grier in the very beginning of this
century, was where he received his early instruction, and he
never forgot his alma mater.

From Northumberland he removed to Baltimore about
1840, and soon afterwards became president of the Tide
Water Canal Company.   In the course of a few years, during which time he had almost entirely relinquished the
practice of his profession, he retired, and removing to Philadelphia, again resumed the law.   He gave close attention to

his profession and soon built up a good practice. In 1855 Governor Pollock appointed him State Law Reporter, and the first 182 pages of I. Casey (Pennsylvania Reports, Vol. XXV.,) were compiled by him, with the exception of three cases. In less than a year after his appointment he fell ill and died, as stated above, in the 66th year of his age.

James Hepburn married, January 29, 1810, Maria Hiatt, and they had issue, all born in Northumberland:

    i. *Mary*, b. November 19, 1811; m. Anson V. Parsons April 3, 1829, and d. September 7, 1856, in Philadelphia.

    ii. *James*, b. August 17, 1813; d. in Williamsport February 19, 1837.

    iii. *Hiatt Park*, b. February 16, 1815. Graduated at Dickinson Law School in 1836, and was admitted to the bar of Cumberland County. Practiced law first in Baltimore, and in 1849 went to California and became a leading lawyer in San Francisco. He m. Susan, sister of Hon. William Preston, of Louisville, Kentucky; returned to California, but d. while on a visit to Louisville May 1, 1864. His widow now lives in Louisville.

    iv. *Sarah Jane*, b. June 7, 1816; m. J. H. Carter, of Baltimore, March 2, 1841, and d. in Harrisburg, Pa., May 11, 1842.

    v. *Ann Eliza*, b. June 20, 1818; m. Edward King, of Philadelphia, and d. in Baltimore January, 1845.

    vi. *Harriet*, b. November 19, 1821; m. Henry Wilkins and removed to California; lives at San Rafael. Issue: Henry Wilkins, now a member of the bar, San Rafael; James Hepburn Wilkins, journalist, and editor of a paper in San Rafael.

    vii. *Lydia Louisa*, b. April 19, 1828; d. September 29, 1829, in Northumberland.

    viii. *Emma Maria*, b. October 9, 1831; d. in San Rafael, California, August 26, 1892, unmarried.

    ix. *Caroline*, b. June 16, 1835; m. Henry McCrea October 20, 1859; d. in Philadelphia April 15, 1891. Issue: 1. Henry McCrea, now a clergyman in New Haven, Connecticut. 2. Maria Hepburn McCrea; lives in New Haven; unmarried.

IX. JANE HEPBURN,[3] (James,[2] Samuel,[1]) born March 19, 1795, was the sixth child and eldest daughter of James and Mary Hopewell Hepburn; married Francis C. Campbell, of Williamsport, May, 1816; died May 19, 1867.

Mr. Campbell, born at York, Pa., April 18, 1787, graduated at Dickinson College and became a man of high literary attainments. His father, John Campbell, studied
theology, and desiring to attach himself to the Protestant
Episcopal Church, went to England for ordination, there
not being at this time any bishop of this church in America. He was ordained by the Bishop of London, and was for
some years rector of All-Saints' Church, Hertford, County
Middlesex, England. He there married Miss Catharine Cut-
ler, daughter of the mayor of the town in which his charge
was situated. On the urgent request of his father, who was
then living in this country, he returned to Pennsylvania,
where, as his tombstone in the cemetery at Carlisle informs
us, he was for " more than thirty years rector of St. John's
Protestant Episcopal Church at Carlisle."

After leaving Dickinson College Francis studied law under the direction of David Watts, Esq., an eminent lawyer
of Carlisle, and was admitted to the bar in August, 1810.
He located in Williamsport April 18, 1812, being then just
past twenty-five years of age. He married Miss Hepburn
at the residence of her parents in Northumberland in May,
1816, and the young couple immediately took up their residence in Williamsport, which was then a very small village.
Mr. Campbell was among the early lawyers to settle in the
infant town, but he soon took a leading rank at the bar and
speedily built up a fine practice. He stood high among the
lawyers of the State for his legal attainments, and his practice was marked by great success. He devoted himself exclusively to his profession, refusing all political preferment,
and was in active practice for fifty years, when he retired,
commanding the respect of his contemporaries and a wide
circle of friends. His integrity was above suspicion, and
his reputation for learning, honesty, benevolence and good
works, remains as a legacy of honor to his posterity, and his
memory is cherished as one largely endowed by nature

with every virtue, who passed through the activities of a long and successful career. He died April 21, 1867, in the 81st year of his age, and his wife followed him May 19, 1867, in her 73d year. They had issue (surname Campbell) :

 i. *Mary Jane*, b, 1817; m., 1836, Robert Faries, civil engineer; d. May 24, 1849. They had seven children. Robert H. Faries, civil engineer, Williamsport, is one of the number.

 ii. *John Richard*, b. September 5, 1818; m. Elizabeth, daughter of the late Judge Anthony; d. in Washington, D. C., September 23, 1892.

 iii. *James Hepburn*, b. February 8, 1820. Graduated from Carlisle Law School and was admitted to the bar in 1841; m. Juliet, daughter of the late Chief Justice Ellis Lewis of the Supreme Court; settled in Pottsville, Pa., and represented that district in Congress from 1855 to 1857, and again from 1858 to 1861; in 1864 appointed Minister to Sweden by Mr. Lincoln; in 1866 appointed Minister to Bogota by Mr. Johnson, but declined. Resides at Wayne, Delaware County, Pa.

 iv. *Catherine C.*, b.———; m., first, John F. Carter; second, Lewis Jamison; widow; resides in Washington, D. C.

 v. *Caroline L.*, b.———; m. Rev. J. H. Black; widow; resides in Washington, D. C.

 vi. *Washington Lee*, b.———; deceased.

 vii. *Elizabeth*, b.———; m. S. W. Gear; both deceased.

 viii. *Sarah C.*, b.———; m., first, Capt. N. Ruggles; second, Judge Stanbury, St. Augustine, Florida; resides there; widow.

 ix. *Frank H.*, b.———; deceased.

 x. *Alfred*, b.———; deceased.

X. MARY HEPBURN,[3] (James,[2] Samuel,[1]) eighth child and second daughter of James and Mary Hopewell Hepburn, was born May 6, 1797, at Northumberland. She married James Merrill, of New Berlin, Union County, Pa., November 13, 1821, and died June 5, 1825, leaving two children— Charles and Mary Jane—surname Merrill. Charles, born November 17, 1824, died at Nashville, Tennessee, November, 1865; Mary Jane, married Col. A. L. Hough, U. S. A., February 11, 1857. Mr. Merrill married, secondly, Sarah, widow of Samuel Hepburn, (son of Judge William Hepburn, of Williamsport,) who died in August, 1824. She was a daughter of John Cowden, and died September 17, 1831, leaving one son, George. Mr. Merrill married, thirdly, Miss Sarah B. Lewis, and he died October 29, 1841, at the early age of 52, leaving two sons, viz.: Gen. Lewis Merrill, U. S. A., and Gen. Jesse Merrill, a well known member of the bar, Lock Haven, Pa. The mother of these two sons, Mrs. Sarah B. (nee Lewis), died August 4, 1876, aged 82.

James Merrill, Esq., born in Vermont May 8, 1790, graduated at Dartmouth College in 1812; studied law under David Cassatt, Esq., of York, Pa. Settled at New Berlin, Pa., and in 1817 was postmaster of the village; 1821–1824 served as deputy attorney general of the county (Union), and was chosen senatorial delegate to the Constitutional Convention of 1837–38, in which he took a prominent and effective part. He attained distinction at the bar and commanded the respect and admiration of such men as Thaddeus Stevens, Ingersoll, Woodward and Dunlop.

XI. HOPEWELL HEPBURN,[3] (James,[2] Samuel,[1]) born at Northumberland, Pa., October 28, 1799, was the seventh child and sixth son of James and Mary Hopewell Hepburn, of that place. In his youth he attended the academy taught by R. C. Grier, where their acquaintance began, which probably led to his appointment as Judge Grier's associate. He graduated from Princeton College; read law with his brother, Samuel Hepburn, at Milton, Pa., and was admitted to the bar at Easton in 1822 or 1823. He soon after settled at Easton, Pa., where he engaged in the practice of his profession. There he married Miss Caroline, daughter of Lawrence Cauffman, of Philadelphia.

Mr. Hepburn followed his profession at Easton until appointed Associate Judge of the District Court at Pittsburg, September 17, 1844, and removed to that city. When Judge Grier was advanced to the Supreme Court of the

JUDGE HOPEWELL HEPBURN

BORN OCTOBER 28TH, 1799   DIED FEBRUARY 14TH, 1863

United States, he was commissioned as President Judge, August 13, 1846, by Governor Shunk, and held that position until November 3, 1851, when he resigned on account of politics. The first election of judges was in October, 1851, under the amended Constitution of 1850. He had been on the bench of the District Court for seven years, and had given entire satisfaction to the people and bar by his promptness in the dispatch of business, his fidelity to duty, his integrity, learning and legal ability. His qualifications and fitness for the position were acknowledged by all, but he was a Democrat, and the office had become elective. Party lines were drawn. The Democrats nominated Hepburn and the Whigs, Walter Forward; and the Whigs, having a majority, elected their man.

After Judge Hepburn retired from the bench he practiced law at Pittsburg for a few years, then withdrew from the practice, accepting the presidency of the Allegheny Bank, which he held for three years. His health having failed, he removed to Philadelphia and died there February 14, 1863. His wife died August 20, 1879. They had issue :

    i. Mary Elizabeth, m. L. Clarkson Wilmarth, of Pittsburg.
    ii. Sarah Cauffman.
    iii. Lawrence Cauffman, m. Sarah E., daughter of David Wagener, of Easton; d. in August, 1885.
    iv. James Francis, d. May 1, 1856.
    v. Julia, d. in infancy.
    vi. Elena Maria.

With the death of the last of the above three surviving sisters the Hopewell Hepburn branch becomes extinct.

XII. SARAH HEPBURN,[3] (James,[2] Samuel,[1]) ninth child and youngest daughter of James and Mary Hopewell Hepburn, of Northumberland, born September 10, 1801; married James Armstrong, and died at Williamsport February 20, 1829.

Hon. James Armstrong, born at Milton February 15,

1794, settled at Williamsport when a young man, read law under the direction of Hon. Joseph B. Anthony and was admitted to the bar sometime towards the close of the first quarter of the nineteenth century. He gave close attention to his profession and soon built up a fine practice. April 6, 1857, he was appointed by Gov. James Pollock to a position on the Supreme Bench of the State, to fill a vacancy caused by the resignation of Judge Jeremiah S. Black, and served until December, 1857, when he retired and declined a renomination. Judge Armstrong never remarried, but remained a widower until his death (over thirty-five years), which occurred August 13, 1867, in the 74th year of his age. He is buried by the side of his young wife in the Williamsport Cemetery, and a neat monument marks their graves. They left issue (surname Armstrong):

> *i.* *William Hepburn*, b. September 7, 1824; graduated at Princeton College in 1847; adopted the profession of the law; was elected to the State Legislature in 1860 and 1861; elected a Representative from the XVIth Pennsylvania district to the Forty-first Congress, serving on the committees on Indian Affairs and the Civil Service; in 1882 was appointed by President Arthur Commissioner of Railroads in the Department of the Interior. Is retired and lives in Philadelphia.
>
> *ii.* *Mary H.*, resides in Chicago.
>
> *iii.* *Sarah Pollock*, m. H. L. Holden; resides in Chicago.

MARY HEPBURN, first daughter and eldest child of James and Maria Hiatt Hepburn, married Anson V. Parsons, April 3, 1829, and died September 7, 1856, in the 45th year of her age.

Hon. Anson Virgil Parsons was born in Granville, Massachusetts, in 1798. After a thorough course in the schools of his native town, he entered the Law School at Litchfield, Connecticut, and was graduated therefrom with high honors. He then came to Pennsylvania and stopped for a short time at Lancaster for the purpose of familiarizing himself with

A. N. Parsons

Pennsylvania state practice in the office of Andrew Porter, Esq. Thence he made his way up the valley of the Susquehanna in search of a place in which to locate. Selecting Jersey Shore, then a promising little town in Lycoming County, he there opened an office in 1824 and became the first lawyer in the place. He remained there till sometime in 1834, when he removed to Williamsport, as the county seat offered better opportunities for the practice of his profession.

By close attention to his profession Mr. Parsons soon acquired a good practice and built up a fine reputation. One of his contemporaries said of him: " No one at the Williamsport bar could gain the attention of a jury more quickly and retain it longer than Mr. Parsons. He studied the evidence in his cases very thoroughly before they came to trial, therefore he was prepared to make strong and convincing arguments and secure the admission of his own evidence and the rejection of much that was offered by opposing counsel."

March 5, 1839, he was chosen State Senator to fill the vacancy caused by the resignation of Alexander Irvin the preceding month. The senatorial district at that time was composed of the counties of Centre, Clearfield, Lycoming, Potter and McKean. The local contest at that time was the formation of the new county of Clinton, which was advocated by the eccentric Jerry Church; and notwithstanding Senator Parsons was elected through the influence of the party opposed to the erection of Clinton, Church won the fight.

On the 22d of January, 1843, Governor Porter appointed Mr. Parsons Secretary of the Commonwealth, and he discharged the responsible duties of that office until the 16th of February, 1844, when he retired to accept the appointment of President Judge of the Court of Common Pleas, Philadelphia, and removed to that city. At the end of his term he remained there and resumed the practice of his profession. During his residence in Philadelphia, Judge Parsons published, in two volumes, a valuable collection of decisions, entitled "Parsons' Equity Cases," which is regarded as a standard work by the profession.

In 1853 Judge Parsons had the misfortune to lose his wife by death. He continued his residence in Philadelphia until his death, which occurred in September, 1882, at the age of 83 years. Judge Parsons and Mary Hepburn, his wife, had issue (surname Parsons):

> i. *Henry C.*, b. in Jersey Shore February 10, 1834. (See sketch following No. 31.)
> ii. *Emma*, b.———; m. Howard Richmond, and lives in Providence, R. I.
> iii. *Elizabeth C.*, b.———; lives in San Rafael, California; unmarried.
> iv. *Francis Wadsworth*, b.———; editor *San Marin Tocsin*, San Rafael, California; unmarried.

DESCENDANTS OF JUDGE WILLIAM HEPBURN.

XIII. JANET HEPBURN,[3] (William,[2] Samuel,[1]) born August 22, 1778; married Matthew Wilson December 17, 1793, and died July 6, 1811, at the mansion house on the Deer Park farm. She was the eldest child of Judge William Hepburn and his first wife, Crecy Covenhoven, and was born in the darkest and most troublous days in the West Branch Valley—when a savage lurked in every thicket and the settlers had to take refuge in the forts and stockades for protection.

Matthew Wilson was born in the North of Ireland in 1762. Nothing is known of his parentage. He came to America about 1773 or 1774, and settled in Northumberland County. As he entered the army of the Revolution, enlisting in Capt. James Parr's company May 17, 1776, he could only have been about fourteen years old at that time. He served his time and returned home.

That he was interested in a land transaction in Washington Township, now Lycoming County, as early as May 9, 1789, is shown by Deed Book A, p. 115, wherein he "conveys to James Bailey, of Lycoming Township, a warrant named William Grier, No. 607, in consideration of £37 10s."

He married, first, Elizabeth, daughter of Andrew and Janet Boyd Culbertson,* about 1790. She had one child and died soon after its birth. This child, born May 4, 1791, was named Alexander Wilson, and became a prominent business man in Philadelphia. He died in that city October 9, 1866, leaving a second wife, two daughters and one son. The son, Boyd Wilson, now lives in Louisville, Kentucky, and has a family consisting of his wife, two sons and two daughters.

On December 17, 1793, Matthew Wilson married, second, Janet Hepburn.† Soon afterwards they settled eight miles west of Williamsport, in Level Corner. October 7, 1796, Mr. Wilson entered into an article of agreement with Hugh McClane for the purchase of 188 acres and 122 perches, in consideration of the payment of £661 10s. This farm was situated in Lycoming Township, Lycoming County, and adjoined the farm of the celebrated Bratton Caldwell (who lived on Pine Run), and extended to the river. The article of agreement, which is on record at Williamsport, stipulates that he was to give a mortgage in double the amount (£1,323) as security for the price (£661 10s.) agreed on, and the last payment was to fall due Sep-

---

*Andrew Culbertson, b. 1731; m. Janet Boyd, and settled on what is now the site of the borough of DuBoistown, near Williamsport, before the Revolution. He was an active, enterprising man, built a mill, and made other improvements. He died in 1797, and his wife followed him in 1802.

† This very full and interesting history of the descendants of Janet Hepburn Wilson was prepared by Miss Mary M., daughter of Samuel Wilson, of 335 Hudson Street, Buffalo, N. Y.

tember 1, 1801. It nowhere appears that he ever complied with the terms of the agreement.

In 1796 he was assessed in Lycoming Township for " 76 acres cleared land, two horses and five cows." In 1797 he was assessed for " 140 acres cleared land, one house, one barn, four horses, five cows and one still house." The total amount of his assessment was £2 16s. 11d. His name appears on the assessment books until 1809. While living at Level Corner he appears to have kept a store in connection with his farming operations.

He also appears on the assessment books of Loyalsock Township, which then embraced Williamsport, as the owner of 200 acres of land, five of which was cleared, in 1796. It was valued at £50, and in addition he was assessed with " one cabin, value £5." This was a tract of land in which his wife was interested and which was afterwards saved by her father.

On the 25th of August, 1797, Michael Ross, the founder of Williamsport, sold Matthew Wilson " lot No. 186, on the corner of the Diamond, north side, in consideration of £45." This lot is in the north-east corner of the square, and adjoins Kline's hardware store. After 1800 his name does not appear on the assessment book.

Sometime in the fall of 1810, or beginning of 1811, Mr. Wilson went to Pittsburg on business, and was soon afterwards stricken with a fever, from which he died March 10, 1811, and was buried in that city. His wife survived him but a few months, as she died at her father's house July 6, 1811, leaving an infant son, Robert, who was born in Williamsport October 16, 1810, in the house where his mother died.

The five surviving orphan children were all born on the farm at Level Corner, but the youngest, and all were cared for by their grandfather, who afterwards bequeathed to each one the sum of $200 and an equal share in 200 acres of land, which was sold after his death and the proceeds divided among them. Matthew Wilson and wife, Janet Hepburn, had issue (surname Wilson):

 i. William, b. September 19, 1794; d. July 5, 1849.
 ii. James, b. June 8, 1796; d. December 30, 1807.
 iii. Molly, b. May 11, 1799; d. August 27, 1852.
 iv. Samuel, b. August 29, 1801; d. January 12, 1893.
 v. John, b. June 13, 1803; d. December 24, 1807.
 vi. Crecy, b. December 30, 1805; d. December 26, 1807.
 vii. Matilda, b. September 22, 1807; still living.
 viii. James, b. August 14, 1809; d. November 26, 1809.
 ix. Robert, b. October 16, 1810; d. September 26, 1870.

HISTORY OF THE WILSON FAMILY.

William Wilson,* the eldest son, was raised in Williamsport by his grandfather. He learned the trade of a saddle and harness maker and established himself in business in Williamsport, which he carried on for several years. He married Sarah Tallman, of Williamsport, April 26, 1821. She was born April 4, 1801, and died February 24, 1822, leaving an infant son, James Wesley Wilson, born February 4, 1822. He grew to manhood and became a minister of the M. E. Church, and was a member of the East Genesee Conference (afterwards the Genesee Conference) of New York State, in which relation he continued till his death, which occurred a few years ago at Syracuse, New York. He left a widow—formerly Phoebe Phillips—and one son, James William Wilson, now a prominent lawyer in Syracuse. He is married and has two children.

William Wilson married, second, Catherine Kohn. To them were born five children:

 1. Augustus, who is now living with his wife—formerly Emeline Foreman—and only son, Alexander Boyd Wilson, at Turnerville, Gloucester County, N. J.

---

*In those days there were two William Wilsons living in Williamsport— one was a member of Congress, and the other a saddle and harness maker. To designate them the people called one "Saddler Billy"—the other "Congress Billy."

2. Sarah Matilda, now Mrs. Lyman M. Champlin, of Parma, Jackson County, Michigan, and who has one daughter.

3. Joseph Kohn, who became a physician and lived for many years at Alligan, Michigan, but afterwards removed to Kansas, where he d. several years ago. He left a widow (since dead) and several children.

4. Janet M., who d. January 12, 1848.

5. Marmaduke Pearce. He became an artist. In 1868 he m. Maggie Rose, of Buffalo. They had one child, but the mother d. soon after its birth, and Marmaduke survived his wife but three days. Lastly their child d. at the age of four months.

Catherine Kohn, second wife of William Wilson, died in Baltimore County, Maryland, February 25, 1843.

Several years after her death William Wilson married, as his third wife, Sarah Peck, of Nunda, N. Y., where he lived at the time. She had one son and one daughter. The latter died in infancy, but the son, William Seth Wilson, died only a few years ago, leaving a family. His mother has since died. William Wilson, the progenitor, died July 5, 1849, at Nunda, N. Y., in the 55th year of his age, where he was buried.

Molly, the third child, was raised in Williamsport by her grandparents. She married Manning Stevenson, of Lycoming County. They had three children, surname Stevenson, viz.: James, Janet and William. Mrs. Stevenson died August 27, 1852, and her husband and daughter soon after followed her. James Stevenson was living in North Carolina, and William, his brother, was living in California, at last accounts.

A TRADESMAN AND INVENTOR.

Samuel, born August 29, 1801, on his father's farm at Level Corner, Lycoming County, Pa., lived part of the time after his parents' death (in 1811) with his grandfather, and part of the time with his granduncle, Robert Covenhoven, till 1820. On the 5th of May of that year, wishing to learn a trade, he chose his uncle, Robert McClure, as his guardian, who bound him to a blacksmith. He served his full time, three years, but did not follow that trade very long, as he soon went to work for his eldest brother, William, who was then a saddle and harness maker at Williamsport. He worked for his brother till he learned that trade also. After that his brother frequently sent him up into Western and Central New York with loads of harness to sell for him. It was in this way that he first came to Dansville, Livingston County, N. Y., where he had friends, Mr. and Mrs. Samuel Shannon, who were originally from Williamsport. In May, 1826, Samuel went to Dansville and opened a saddle and harness shop, commencing business for himself. He boarded with his old friends, the Shannons. After he had been there about a year a young lady, Miss T. Cordelia Enos, came to Dansville to visit her aunt, Mrs. Jonathan Rowley. Mrs. Shannon becoming acquainted with her, and being greatly pleased with her, said to him one day: "There, Samuel, is a wife for you!" Whether this made any impression on his mind or not, he too sought the acquaintance of Miss Enos, and that acquaintance ripened into an engagement. The young lady spent a happy year in Dansville and returned to her home. So it happened that one day in January, 1829, the young lover left Dansville with a horse and sleigh and drove to Eaton, Madison County, N. Y. There, on January 22, 1829, (in the same house in which the bride was born, August 17, 1808,) Samuel Wilson was married to Thankful Cordelia Enos, eldest daughter of Joseph and Hannah Patterson Enos. The following day the happy pair started back to Dansville. The journey, under other circumstances, would have proved tedious, as a "January thaw" caught them on the way, and they drove into town on bare ground. They commenced

housekeeping at once, and the " home " that was then established has remained unbroken, under whatever roof, in whatever place it has been kept, through all these years till the
present time. Their union proved to be a happy one. Nine
children were born to them, four sons and five daughters.

During the early years of Mr. Wilson's residence in Dansville, his youngest brother, Robert, came and learned the
trade with him. Afterwards his elder brother, William,
(who was at that time a widower,) came to live with him,
and entered into partnership in his business.

With the exception of three or four years spent on his
farm in South Dansville, Steuben County, (five miles from
the village of Dansville,) Samuel continued in the harness
business in Dansville, till the " gold fever " broke out, when
he too was seized by it. On June 20, 1849, in company
with a number of friends, he sailed from New York on the
sailing vessel Probus, bound for San Francisco via Cape
Horn. After a long and tedious voyage, during which
they landed but once—and that was at Valparaiso, Chili,
October 4th—they at last arrived at San Francisco, December 14, 1849. There Mr. Wilson remained till sometime in February, 1851, when he sailed for home via Panama, arriving at New York in March, a month from the
time of sailing.

After a year's stay at home he again started for California;
this time by the Isthmus. After reaching his destination he
went up to the mines of Mariposa, where his eldest son,
James, was living. [The latter had crossed the plains and
had arrived in San Francisco the day after his father had
sailed for home in February, 1851.] He found his son's
cabin, but James was away at the time. Taking possession
of the place, he waited for his son's return. At last he saw
a heavily-bearded man approaching, who proved to be the
son who had left home when a boy of about eighteen years.
A happy meeting it was between father and son, who had

been separated for four years, and after each had gone through so many hardships and faced so many dangers by sea and land.   They both remained in California till the 23d of April, 1853, when they sailed for home via Panama, on the mail steamer, Isthmus.

With the exception of a few months spent in Rockford, Illinois, Mr. Wilson lived in Dansville from the last of May, 1853, till May, 1856, when he went to Buffalo, N. Y., to fill the position of retailer and overseer in one of the large flouring mills situated on the pier at Black Rock.   In this business he remained till the spring of 1881, when he retired from business.   From that time he led a quiet, home life.

Like his brother Robert, Samuel had an inventive brain. While he was in the harness business he invented a saddler's and harness maker's creasing machine, which he had patented, and for which he was awarded a large silver medal at the American Institute in New York, 1845, and the following year a diploma from the same Institute.   These machines for creasing leather he introduced all over the country, and they were the first machines to do the work that had before been done so laboriously by hand.   Then he invented other tools for splitting and shaving leather, &c., to be used in his trade.

When he went into the milling business he soon saw the waste of time and money in the employment of a man to watch the packer and mark down every barrel of flour as it was packed.   Mistakes were frequently made by such tally-men; so his active brain went to work to remedy the defect. The result of this was a "tally machine," or "register" (as he called it).   This machine was attached to a post near the packer, so that when the stem of the packer passed down it pressed a cam, which moved a set of wheels on which were dials that registered, in all, 9,999, the next move changing all the figures to ciphers, announced that 10,000 barrels had been packed, and the next tally would commence at 1. As at the close of each day's work the attendant copied the state of the register on a bulletin board, each day's count was easily ascertained. It was found that the machine was a great improvement on the old way, and it was introduced all over the United States. He applied the same principle to a register to be used in weighing wheat, by attaching it to the hopper. For many years they were the only machines used in the mills for the purpose of registering.

Although Mr. Wilson was so far advanced in years when he retired from business, he was always a very active man after that; constantly looking about to find something with which to busy himself, and to help others around him, except when illness enforced rest, as he was always happiest when busy and aiding others. He was a man of medium height and size; thus he was not enfeebled by over-weight. His ever active brain and energy prompted him to exertions that many a younger man would shrink from. Though his hair, which had been of a light brown color, was thin and white for many years, his complexion was as clear as that of a child. This, with the heightened color of his cheeks and the brightness of his large, dark brown eyes, seemed to deny his years and make old age beautiful. He possessed a nature of extreme firmness, mingled with the greatest gentleness. Devoid of selfishness, he always preferred the happiness and comfort of others to his own. To say that he was respected by those with whom he came in contact, and loved by all who knew him, is no exaggeration. He was especially fond of children and was, in return, loved by them. He never lost his interest in young people and their affairs. He was happy in their society, often entertaining them, and being entertained by them, as usually only those of near age can do; thus bridging the many years that lay between them with a warm sympathy that made him many friends among the young of both sexes. To his friends he never seemed old, as his manner of speaking and actions were those of a young person. Ever quick at repartee, and keenly appreciative of a joke, he was especially companionable to young men, among whom he had many friends.

His memory was good; unlike most aged people who recall the occurrences of the distant past, forgetting those of later years, he seemed to remember almost everything from early youth till the last days of his long and eventful life. He was a great reader, and being familiar with all the current events of the day, he would discuss public matters with any one, with the clearness of perception and soundness of judgment of most men of fifty. He read a paper for the last time on January 1, 1893, but after that, up to the eve of his death, he did not lose interest in public matters, but wished others to tell him the news, as he was unable to read. In his political views he was a staunch Republican, and had always been one since the formation of that party. Before that, from the time he cast his first vote, he was an old-line Whig.

Although he believed in the truths of the Gospel of Christ, he was always reticent about his own experience, his inner life; but his whole outward life was an exemplification of those teachings, and especially of the Golden Rule. He retained his faculties till the last moment of life, when, in the early morning of January 12, 1893, his freed spirit left the poor, worn-out body that had been its habitation for 91 years, 4 months and 13 days, and entered into rest. Like a ripe sheaf of corn in the fullness thereof he was gathered to his fathers. His wife died May 2, 1866, at Buffalo, N. Y., in the 58th year of her age, having preceded him over 26 years. They had issue (surname Wilson):

1. James Hepburn, who is now living in San Francisco. He m. Elizabeth Trickey, New York City, December 22, 1858. She d. in San Francisco February 28, 1886, leaving three daughters, as follows: Kate C., b.

in Tonawanda, N. Y.; m. Thomas P. Deering, at San
Francisco, January 24, 1884. Mr. Deering is first
officer on the steamship Alameda, running between
San Francisco and Australia. Josephine E., b. at
Tonawanda; m. James Niven, at San Francisco, No-
vember 24, 1880, and was left a widow March 26,
1886, with one son and one daughter. Elizabeth
Mary, d. in San Francisco December 21, 1880.

2. Charles Enos, d. at sea July 15, 1852. He had started
on a voyage around Cape Horn to California for his
health. He sailed from New York July 10, 1852,
full of hope that he would be benefited by the voyage
and join his father and brother James, who were then
in California. The sea air was too strong for his
lungs and he died the fifth day out and was buried
in the sea.

3. Hannah Janet, d. at Buffalo, New York, August 10,
1885.

4. George Samuel, m. Margaret A. Connaughty, of Water-
ford, Saratoga County, N. Y., December 15, 1859.
They had one son, Hamilton George Wilson, b. at
Buffalo July 25, 1868. He is living in Buffalo, and
for five years past has been employed in the Erie
County Savings Bank. His father d. October 31,
1888, at Naples, N. Y., and his mother resides there.

5. Cordelia Maria, now living in Buffalo.

6. Mary Matilda, now living in Buffalo.

7. Sarah Enos, d. in infancy.

8. Joseph B., d. in infancy.

9. Josephine E., d. in infancy.

THE ONLY SURVIVOR.

Matilda, the seventh child, born September 22, 1807, at
Level Corner; married, first, the Rev. Peter McEnally, a
member of the Baltimore M. E. Conference, then residing
at Muncy. Mr. McEnally died at Williamsport many years
ago while attending a session of the Conference in that place.
They had issue (surname McEnally):

1. Elizabeth, m. Mr. Patton; now a widow with several
children; lives at Chicago.

2. Mary, deceased.
3. Annie, deceased.
4. Wilson, deceased.
5. Sarah, m. Dr. Joseph Litz ; now a widow, and lives at DuBois, Pa.
6. James, deceased.
7. Manning.

Mrs. McEnally married, second, Josiah Tate, of Clearfield County. He died about one year after their marriage, leaving her a widow for the second time. Since that time she has lived with Mrs. Litz, of DuBois. She is the last survivor of the family of Matthew and Janet Hepburn Wilson, and at the present writing (July, 1894,) is in the 87th year of her age.

THE FLY NET INVENTOR.

Robert, born October 16, 1810, in Williamsport, was only eight months and twenty days old when his mother died, and he was raised by his grandfather. When of sufficient age he went to his brother Samuel, at Dansville, New York, and learned the trade of a saddle and harness maker. In 1844 he returned to Williamsport and worked at his trade for a few years. In 1850 he located in Milton, Pa., where he continued his trade. Being of an inventive turn of mind, like his brother Samuel, in 1856 he devised what is known as the "Wilson fly net" for horses, and had it patented in 1858, and with the machinery invented by him, he engaged largely and profitably in the manufacture of that article. As early as May 27, 1834, Mr. Wilson married Lucetta, daughter of Dr. Henry Heinen, of Milton. She was born August 6, 1814, and died September 2, 1853. In 1863, at the age of fifty-five years, Robert Wilson volunteered and served three months in the defense of his country during the Rebellion. After remaining a widower about ten years he married Mrs. Rebecca Overpeck, at Milton; and died September 20, 1870. His widow survived him several years and died in Indiana. By his first wife Robert Wilson had seven children, of whom two sons and two daughters died in infancy. The three that attained manhood were:

1. William E., b.———; d. at Milton July 15, 1882, leaving a widow and several children.

2. Henry Hepburn, b.———; killed in the battle before Petersburg, Va., July 30, 1864.

3. Reuben Frederick, b.———; d. March 20, 1892, at Denver, Colorado, whither he had gone to seek relief for pulmonary trouble. He married Marian Reid, at Milton, December 20, 1876, who survives with two sons, Robert Marshall and William Walter Wilson.

XIV. MARY HEPBURN,[3] (William,[2] Samuel,[1]) born on the Deer Park farm in 1780, and died December 17, 1839, in Williamsport, was the second child and daughter of Judge William Hepburn and Crecy Covenhoven, his first wife. She married Robert McClure, who was born in Cumberland County February 6, 1772. He graduated from Dickinson College. Roger B. Taney, afterwards Chief Justice of the United States Supreme Court, and Hon. Charles Huston, were among his classmates. He studied law at Carlisle, and after his admission to the bar came to Williamsport about 1795, and located. He and his classmate, Charles Huston, were the two first lawyers to settle in the town which had just been laid out by Michael Ross.

Mr. McClure is described as a "tall, stout man, with a broad ruddy face and a countenance indicative of firmness and deep thought." He built up a fine law practice, and throughout life was noted for his integrity of character and reliability in business matters. He was sent to the lower house of the Legislature in 1822, and re-elected in 1824. In 1827 he was elected a State Senator, but died December 13, 1829. His will, which was dated December 4, 1829, only nine days before his death, mentions his sons, William,

Robert and Hepburn, and appoints them and his wife executors of his estate. In a codicil he bequeathed his law library to his son, Hepburn McClure; also the journals of Congress and the Legislature, together with the Nicholson State Papers. His two farms were willed to his wife. One was located near Linden, and the other east of Williamsport.

Hepburn McClure, their second son, born November 24, 1809, and died in the spring of 1890, was the oldest living member of the Williamsport bar at the time of his death, having been admitted in 1830. He served as postmaster of Williamsport from May, 1839, to July, 1841, and as prothonotary of Lycoming County from 1842 to 1845. He was also clerk of the United States Court for the Western District of Pennsylvania for many years.

Edward C. McClure, the youngest son, born December 25, 1825, settled in Lock Haven in 1867 and became a member of the banking house of Moore, Simpson & Company. He married Louisa Harriet, daughter of Samuel Hepburn, of Lock Haven, and died in that city January 17, 1890. His widow survives.

There were two daughters, Mary and Louisa. The former married Samuel Lloyd, and the latter Elias Lowe.

XV. SARAH HEPBURN,[3] (William,[2] Samuel,[1]) born 1788, sixth child of Judge William Hepburn by his first marriage. But little is known of her history. She married Alexander Cummings, a young officer in the United States Army and spent most of her married life with her husband at different posts on the frontiers. The date of her death is unknown, but it is supposed to have occurred sometime in the latter part of the thirties. She was living in 1833, at Tampa Bay, Florida, for in that year she affixed her name to a deed for the conveyance of a piece of land in Williamsport. It is probable that she died and was buried in Florida. She had a son and a daughter.

Alexander Cummings came of an old Irish family. His parents were among the early prominent settlers in Lycoming County. He had several brothers, among whom was John Cummings, who became the second sheriff of Lycoming County, and was re-elected several times. Another brother, James, was the father of A. Boyd Cummings, who bequeathed the fine body of land worth $75,000, and now known as " Brandon Park," to the city of Williamsport.

Alexander Cummings, who was an uncle of A. Boyd Cummings, was born in County Tyrone, Ireland, probably about 1776 or 1778, and was quite a young man when he came to Lycoming County. May 3, 1808, he was appointed 2d Lieutenant of the regiment of light dragoons; promoted 1st Lieutenant, September 30, 1809; Captain, November 1, 1811; was transferred to the 4th Infantry, upon the reorganization of the army, May 17, 1815; promoted Major, 3d Infantry, April 20, 1819; Lieutenant Colonel 2d Infantry, August 20, 1828, and Colonel 4th Infantry, December 1, 1839. He died January 21, 1842, in New York City, aged, probably, about sixty or sixty-two years. His wife, according to family tradition, died first.

Colonel Cummings saw much frontier service, besides participating in the war of 1812–14, when he bore the rank of Captain. While stationed at Tampa Bay he had occasion to execute a power of attorney (see Will Book A, p. 161,) to Hepburn McClure to satisfy a mortgage against Robert McClure, his brother-in-law, for $400. The instrument bears this curious indorsement:

Acknowledged before me at my wigwam in the cove of the Ouithlacooche, this 24th day of April, 1839.

FAUS-WA-YA-HA-LOOCHIE,
Chief of the Talahassus

XVI. DR. JAMES HEPBURN,[3] (William,[2] Samuel,[1]) born April 14, 1799, son of William and Crecy Covenhoven Hepburn; died January 21, 1878. He was the tenth and youngest child by his father's first marriage, and lacked six days of being one year old when his mother died. His father married soon again and he was raised by a step-mother. His birthplace was the old log house which stood on the Deer Park farm near where the present brick house, now rapidly falling into ruin, stands.

He received such education as the times afforded, and at the age of nineteen engaged in the study of medicine under the direction of Dr. William R. Power, his brother-in-law, and graduated from the Pennsylvania University in 1823. In 1824 he began the practice of medicine in Williamsport, and followed it until 1837.

On the 1st of June, 1831, as the sole surviving executor of his father's will, he sold to his brother Charles, (Deed Book 20, p. 7,) in consideration of $4,438.75, 110 acres and 155 perches off the Deer Park estate (including the mansion house, foot of Park Street), and the two islands * in the river, called "Hepburn's Islands," containing 10 acres and 140 perches.

Sometime in 1832 he conceived the idea of establishing an iron foundry in Williamsport. Having received the promise of assistance to establish the enterprise, he visited Geneva that winter and made a proposition to John B. Hall, a practical iron worker, to come to Williamsport and take charge of the foundry, in connection with Tunison Coryell

---

* These islands were applied for by Frederick Hineman, Jr., and by him conveyed to Alexander Scott, who sold them to William Hepburn. By reference to Deed Book No. 23, p. 123, it will be seen that on December 1, 1836, Charles Hepburn sold 114 acres and 36 perches of the Deer Park farm to Matthew C. Ralston, of Philadelphia, for $14,509, an advance of $10,070.25 over what he paid for it five years before.

and himself. Gaining his consent, the Doctor returned to Williamsport and selected a lot for the foundry, whereon a frame building 40 x 60 feet was erected. It stood within a few yards of the south side of the magnificent City Hall building, which was dedicated July 4, 1894. In the meantime Mr. Hall had his engine, boilers and cupola transported from Geneva to Williamsport by wagons, and by the beginning of September, 1832, he was ready and made the first castings. This was the *first* foundry in Lycoming, Tioga, Centre or Bradford counties. Hall brought the first patterns to the town for coal stoves, and made and sold all stoves used in town, and for fifty miles around, for many years. The novelty of the enterprise attracted much attention, and crowds of people visited the foundry on casting days. The moss-backs shook their heads ominously—for there were moss-backs in those days as well as now—and did all they could to discourage the young men who had invested their means in the enterprise. The firm met with many discouragements. Dr. Hepburn lost his means in an iron furnace in Centre County, and had to dispose of his interest in the foundry to John H. Cowden, his father-in-law, who became a partner. Hall, Coryell and Cowden struggled along and finally succeeded. In 1842 Hall purchased the interest of his two partners and assumed control, and in course of time built up a large business. And to-day he is the sole survivor of the pioneer iron founders in Williamsport.

After his retirement from the iron business Dr. Hepburn turned his attention to contracting for the erection of public works. Among them was the reconstruction of the Croton Dam for the water supply of New York, which had given way with heavy damage. It was a gigantic undertaking for the time, the granite having to be transported from Massachusetts, and six hundred laborers were employed at one time on the work. When finished it was regarded as a masterpiece of beauty and strength. In the vicinity an imposing monument of Italian marble was erected, bearing the names of the water commissioners, engineers and contractors, and among them appeared the name of Dr. James Hepburn.

When the California gold fever broke out Dr. Hepburn turned his face toward the new Eldorado in the early fifties. He resided in California about twenty-six years, spending a portion of the time among the mines, and a portion in the practice of his profession. In 1875 he returned to Williamsport an old man, but so many changes had taken place during his absence that he scarcely recognized the home of his early manhood, and he felt that he was a veritable Rip Van Winkle. He fell ill at the home of his half-brother, Huston, and died in his 79th year.

Dr. James Hepburn married, first, Rebecca Cowden, in 1822, and they had issue:

    i. Clara, b.———, 1824; d.———, 1894.

    ii. William Henry, b.———; d.———.

    iii. Sarah, d. young.

    iv. John, b.———; d.———.

    v. Annie C., b.———, 1834; m. Frederick Lovejoy; * he d. November 3, 1894, at the Gilsey House, New York, from the effects of paralysis.

    vi. Mary H., b. ———, 1837; m. Franklin Reading, Williamsport, May 14, 1861. Mr. Reading d. May 31, 1891, leaving a widow, two sons and one daughter. Mrs. Reading now lives in Washington, D. C.

    vii. James, b.———, 1839; d.———.

---

* Frederick Lovejoy was born in Owego, N. Y., in 1836, and had been connected with the express business ever since 1854, when he went to Elmira, N. Y., in the employ of the International Express Company. With that company he first went to Philadelphia in 1857, and when the International Company sold out to Howard & Co.'s Express Mr. Lovejoy was made cashier and general superintendent of the latter concern. Then the Howard & Co.'s Express was absorbed by the Adams Express Company and Mr. Lovejoy remained in the service and rose step by step until in 1877 he became assistant gen-

Mrs. Rebecca Cowden Hepburn (b. 1797 or 1798) died in May, 1839, and Dr. Hepburn married, second, Miss Julia M. Baldwin, of Elmira, N. Y., April 15, 1845. She was born at Elmira March 6, 1819, and died at Mokelumne Hill, California, January 5, 1871. They had issue:

    i. Julia Baldwin, b. at Elmira December 2, 1846; d. near West Point, N. Y., August 2, 1848.

    ii. Stella C., b. at Elmira July 21, 1852; d. at Mokelumne Hill, California, October 14, 1872.

    iii. Susan H., b. at Mokelumne Hill, August 13, 1857; m. John M. Diven, at Elmira, N. Y., November 6, 1878. They have issue (surname Diven): 1. Julia, b. at Elmira December 19, 1879; d. July 11, 1881. 2. Alice, b. at Watkins, N. Y., May 2, 1882. 3. May, b. at Elmira August 23, 1885; d. June 7, 1887. 4. John M., Jr., b. at Elmira May 11, 1890.

XVII. CRECY HEPBURN,[3] (William,[2] Samuel,[1]) born on the Deer Park farm October 1, 1801; married to Thomas Plunket Simmons December 6, 1824, by Rev. McGee, of the Baltimore Conference, and died August 8, 1884, in Williamsport.

Mr. Simmons, who came of an old family, was born in Buffalo Valley April 24, 1798. His mother, Margaret Plunket, was a daughter of Robert, a brother of the celebrated Dr. William Plunket, of Sunbury. Robert and his

---

eral superintendent of the company. Subsequently he was made superintendent of the Pennsylvania division, with headquarters in Philadelphia, a position which he resigned to accept the presidency of the Denver and Rio Grande Railroad in 1884. He only retained this office for a period of nine months, and in 1885 retired from active business and lived quietly in New York for six years. On the reorganization of the Adams Express Company in October, 1891, after the deposition of the late John Hoey from the presidency, Mr. Lovejoy was elected vice-president and general manager, Henry Sanford accepting the presidency on the condition that he was not to be burdened with the details of the business. Mr. Lovejoy had an extensive and intimate knowledge of the express business, and was universally popular with the employes of the company.

family came from Ireland sometime during the Revolutionary war, or before it commenced, and he selected a tract of 300 acres just west of Pine Creek, when it was yet "Indian land," and made an improvement as early as 1778 or 1779.

It is probable that the family of Robert Plunket lived in Buffalo Valley in early times. Samuel Maclay, a prominent man in those days, lived a short distance west of what is now the borough of Lewisburg. His wife, Elizabeth, was a daughter of Dr. William Plunket, of Sunbury, and therefore a niece of Robert Plunket. His daughter, Margaret, born in Ireland in 1760, married Samuel Simmons while they were living near Maclay's, and there their second son, Thomas P., was born, as stated above.

Robert Plunket, it appears, died intestate sometime in 1779, for on the 1st of November of that year letters of administration were issued to his brother, Dr. William Plunket. A warrant of survey was also granted to Dr. Plunket for the land on which his brother had made an improvement before 1780, on the 24th of October, 1784, and he secured the land and held it in trust for the widow and her children. On the 25th of March, 1793, they conveyed their interest in the land to Thomas Grant and Isaac Richardson. The latter, who lived in York County, was married to Margaret, daughter of Dr. William Plunket.

Samuel Simmons and his wife Margaret, being heirs to one-fifth of the estate, he purchased the farm (Deed Book 6, p. 112,) of Grant and Richardson, July 25, 1801, in consideration of £430 5s., and that was the beginning of the well-known Simmons farm on Pine Creek. In the deed one acre was reserved for the Presbyterian Church, which had been built a few years before and stood near the bank of the creek on the north side of the public road.

Samuel Simmons and wife settled on the farm, and there they raised their family. He was born in Ireland in 1765,

and died September 3, 1818, in his 53d year, but his wife*
survived him until March 10, 1835, dying in her 75th year.
The farm is still owned by their descendants.

Samuel Simmons, their eldest son, remained on the farm
and died there September 4, 1856. His wife, Ann Smith,
had preceded him August 8, 1843, in her 48th year.

Thomas P. Simmons, the second son, early became a merchant, and in partnership with Henry Sproul, kept a store in
Newberry for many years. Afterwards he removed to Jersey
Shore, where he continued the mercantile business alone for
some time. During the war he was residing in Williamsport
and served as internal revenue assessor under George Bubb,
who was the government collector at that time. He died November 9, 1871. Mr. Simmons and wife had issue (surname
Simmons) :

    i. Elizabeth Huston, b. January 18, 1827; m. M. J. Wil-
        son, of Centre County, December 18, 1850, and d.
        November 17, 1851, leaving one son, T. P. S. Wilson,
        b. November 5, 1851. Mr. Wilson has charge of the
        City Mission, Williamsport, and has served as a mis-
        sionary among the poor and lowly for many years.
    ii. Margaret Plunket, d. in infancy.
   iii. Charlotte Hepburn, b. June 9, 1836; m. George Slate
        February 19, 1861; has one daughter, Crecy, b.
        February 22, 1862. She m. H. L. Simmons (no
        relation) October 15, 1885, and has issue: 1. George
        Slate Simmons, b. September 1, 1887. 2. Charlotte

---

    *She evidently was a woman of good executive ability. In her will (Book
1, p. 257,) she devised half of the farm, under certain conditions, to her sons
Samuel and Thomas P. Her other children were also provided for. They
were as follows: Anna C., intermarried with Samuel Torbert; Robert P. Simmons; Susan, intermarried with Isaac Torbert, and Elizabeth, intermarried
with William St. Clair. The personal property was divided among the three
daughters, excepting the clock, which she directed to be sold and the money
used in "buying and lettering" a set of silver teaspoons for each of her
granddaughters, viz.: Elizabeth K. Torbert, Margaret S. Torbert, Susan S. St.
Clair, Margaret S. St. Clair, Elizabeth H. Simmons and Margaret P. Simmons.
The will was made February 28, 1834, and probated March 16, 1835.

Hepburn Simmons, b. February 10, 1889. They reside in Brooklyn, N. Y., where Mr. Simmons is secretary of the Y. M. C. A. George Slate, the grandfather of these children, d. December 11, 1889. Mrs. Slate also has one son, William Hepburn, b. March 13, 1866. On the 14th of June, 1894, he m. Nellie Cameron, daughter of the late Hon. John B. Packer, of Sunbury. They reside in Bloomsburg, Pa., where Mr. Slate is engaged in the book and stationery business.

Among the relics preserved of her grandfather, Judge William Hepburn, Mrs. Charlotte Slate has his eight-day clock, made by John Murphy, nearly one hundred years ago. It is yet in running condition and keeps good time. It is a veritable " grandfather's clock."

XVIII. CHARLES HEPBURN,[3] (William,[2] Samuel,[1]) born 1802, in Williamsport, was the first son by the second marriage of Judge William Hepburn, and the second child, and the twelfth counting from the first in the family. He was an active business man during his lifetime. He married Margaret, daughter of William McMeen, born in 1807. Her family settled early on the " Long Reach," west of Williamsport, after having borne a conspicuous part in the Revolutionary struggle, and her father was one of the representative men of his time. She died at Grand Rapids, Michigan, in 1875.

Charles Hepburn purchased, June 1, 1831, of Dr. James Hepburn, then sole surviving executor of his father's estate, (see Deed Book 20, p. 7,) 110 acres and 155 perches of the Deer Park farm, including two islands in the river, containing about 10 acres and 140 perches, in consideration of $4,438.75.

He held this portion of the patrimonial estate until December 1, 1836, when he and his wife conveyed 114 acres and 36 perches (see Deed Book 23, p. 123,) to Matthew C. Ralston, of Philadelphia, in consideration of $14,509.

Mr. Hepburn also erected what is now known as the
"Maynard Mansion," on West Fourth Street, which he sold,
with ninety acres of land, to Judge Maynard, July 22, 1847,
(Deed Book 29,) for ten thousand dollars, and there Mr. Maynard lived until his death in 1885. A descendant still occu-
pies the house.

The records show that during the active years of his life
Charles Hepburn sold and conveyed many lots, until the
Deer Park estate was pretty well divided among strangers.
The Park Hotel, the most elegant public house in Williams-
port, stands on four of these lots. Finally "Major Hep-
burn," as he was familiarly called, moved west and settled at
Grand Rapids, Michigan, where he died in 1877, and is
there buried by the side of his wife. They had issue:

 i. Elizabeth, m. George Voorhis and lives in Grand Rapids.
 ii. William, m. and lives in Oregon.
 iii. John, m. and lives in California.
 iv. Augustus, m. and lives in Grand Rapids.
 v. Mercy Power, m. Edward Montgomery and lives in Grand Rapids.
 vi. Samuel, m. and lives in Kansas.

XIX. HARRIET HEPBURN,[3] (William,[2] Samuel,[1]) was born
November 23, 1804, in the infant settlement of Williamsport, on the Deer Park farm. She was the thirteenth child
of Judge Hepburn, and the third by his second marriage.
She became the second wife of Dr. E. L. Hart, a noted physician of Elmira, November 1, 1843, and died August 6,
1892, aged 87 years, 8 months and 13 days. Next to her
grandfather, she reached the greatest age of any of his descendants up to the present time.

Mrs. Harriet Hepburn Hart left one son, Charles Lang-
don Hart, born April 10, 1845. He married Fanny Richardson Smith, of Elmira, June 18, 1879. She was born
September 19, 1855. Their only child, Charles Earle Hart,
was born March 5, 1881. They reside in Elmira.

Dr. E. L. Hart, who was born in Goshen, Connecticut,

May 8, 1787, died in Elmira October 23, 1871, and was therefore seventeen years older than his second wife. He was a popular physician in his time, but entertained some peculiar prejudices regarding modes of transportation. For instance, it is related of him that he could not be induced to enter a railway car, and when he had occasion to visit Williamsport he always drove overland in his carriage.

XX. JOHN HEPBURN,[3] (William,[2] Samuel,[1]) born in Williamsport November 16, 1806; married Caroline Wheeler, Elmira, March 8, 1831. She was born June 6, 1807; died August 24, 1878. Mr. Hepburn died November 24, 1878.

He was raised on his father's farm, known as Deer Park, and received such a rudimentary education as the schools of the time afforded. He learned the trade of a saddle and harness maker, and in partnership with his brother, Cowden, carried on the business for a number of years in Elmira. Failing in health, he abandoned his trade and became a farmer. After a time he returned to Williamsport, where he continued to reside until his death.

In 1867 he was elected an alderman for the Third Ward, Williamsport, and was commissioned June 10, 1867, by Governor Geary, to serve five years from that date. He was re-elected for the third time and died in office. John Hepburn and his wife Caroline had issue :

> i. *Elizabeth*, b. February 8, 1832; m. Valentine S. Doebler February 17, 1853.

Mr. Doebler was proprietor of the United States Hotel, Williamsport, one of the most popular public houses of its time, for many years. He died, suddenly, after an illness of only seventeen hours, October 17, 1866, in the fortieth year of his age. They had issue (surname Doebler):

1. Mary Caroline, b. May 28, 1854; m. Rev. Peter Baldy Lightner, of the Episcopal Church, and they reside in Denver, Colorado. Have had three daughters; two deceased.

2. Margaret Biggs, b. January 7, 1855; m. George Meredith Ball, general manager of the Empire Line, Philadelphia; have five sons and two daughters.

3. Mercy Ann, b. December 8, 1857; unmarried.

4. Charles Hay, b. March 17, 1860; m. Pauline Ward, of Fort Wayne, Indiana. They reside in Wabash, Indiana, where Mr. Doebler is master mechanic, Michigan Division, "Big Four" Railroad system. Have one daughter.

5. John Hepburn, b. November 22, 1861; m. Camilla Heulings; live in Philadelphia; no issue.

6. Elizabeth, b. December 30, 1863; m. Herbert Ide Keen; live in Philadelphia; have one daughter.

7. Valentine Sherman, b. December 1, 1865; unmarried; resides in Hollidaysburg; civil engineer by profession.

> *ii. William E.*, b. March 11, 1834; m. Helen Elizabeth Post, of Elmira. No issue.

In 1854 Mr. Hepburn commenced service on the Northern Central Railroad as a brakeman between Williamsport and Elmira, and gradually worked himself up to the position of conductor, and ran in that line of duty from 1860 to 1865. In 1867, soon after the death of his brother-in-law, V. S. Doebler, he opened a hotel in Williamsport and called it the "Hepburn House." It was located on the corner of West Fourth and Pine streets, and soon became a popular place of resort. He conducted the hotel until 1874, when he retired to resume his old business of railroading, and accepting a conductorship on the New York, Lake Erie and Western Railroad, has been running between Binghamton and Jersey City since that time, a distance of 215 miles. For several years he has had charge of the fast train known as the Limited Express.

> *iii. Albert Huston*, b. August 29, 1836; m. Emma Dobbins, of Troy, Pa. Reside in Elmira; have one son, John William Hepburn.
>
> *iv. Mercy Anna*, b. March 25, 1839; m. Edson Avery Tinker October 13, 1869.

Mr. Tinker was engaged in the hotel business for many years. At one time he was interested in the old City Hotel,

Williamsport; afterwards he kept the Jones House (now The Commonwealth), Harrisburg, for several years. For four or five years he has been manager of the dining rooms in the Pennsylvania Railroad Station, Harrisburg. They have issue (surname Tinker):

1. John Hepburn, b. July 28, 1870.
2. Martin Powell, b. November 29, 1873.

> *v. Charles John,** b. July 4, 1841; m. Georgie M. Taylor, of Williamsport, in 1865.

In 1857 he commenced service as a telegraph operator on the Elmira and Williamsport Railroad; in 1859 he went with the Sunbury and Erie, now a part of the Pennsylvania Railroad system, in the same capacity. Sometime in 1860 he was made train despatcher, and in 1861 he was promoted to division operator. In 1866 he was appointed despatcher on the Allegheny and Great Western Railroad at Meadville. One year afterwards (1867) he became train master on the Warren and Franklin Railroad, and before the close of the year he was appointed superintendent. This position he held until he was made general superintendent of the Pittsburg, Titusville and Buffalo Railroad, of which the Warren and Franklin was part by consolidation. During the years 1879–1881 Mr. Hepburn was engaged in building an oil pipe line from Olean to New York City. Having finished this great work, he returned to railroading as superintendent of the Evansville and Terre Haute Railroad, and the same year (1881) he was appointed general superintendent of the same road and branch lines; and at the same time he was made receiver of the Indianapolis and Evansville Railroad, and held both positions until 1883. He was then appointed general superintendent of the Cincinnati, Hamilton and Dayton Railroad, at Cincinnati, which position he held until 1884, when he was taken sick and has been unable to attend to business since. For more than twenty-five years the life of Mr. Hepburn was one of great activity, and he rose rapidly in the line of his profession. Had it not been for his misfortune in being stricken down by disease he would undoubtedly have attained to a much higher distinction as a railroad officer.

* So far as known, Mr. Hepburn is the only one of the name who enjoys the distinction of being born on the natal day of American independence.

Mr. Hepburn is now a resident of the city of Erie, Pa. Issue: 1. Fred. Taylor, born at Corry in 1873. Graduated from Rensselaer Polytechnic Institute, Troy, New York, in 1893, as a civil engineer, and is now in the employ of the Pennsylvania Railroad Company at Erie, Pa., in the engineering department.   2. Clarence Wheeler.

> *vi. Clarence Wheeler*, b. August 22, 1845; d. in infancy.
>
> *vii. Caroline Emily*, b. May 15, 1847; m., first, Martin Powell, and had issue (surname Powell): George, d. in infancy; Caroline and Elizabeth.

Mr. Powell was for a short time in the banking business in Williamsport. He served as mayor of the city in 1874 and 1875, and died at Bradford, McKean County, May 11, 1879, aged 33.

Mrs. Powell married, second, Hon. Amos H. Mylin in February, 1884. Mr. Mylin was born in West Lampeter Township, Lancaster County, September 29, 1837. He was educated at Andover, Massachusetts, and graduated from the law department of the University of Pennsylvania in 1864, and is at present a farmer near Lancaster City. He was a member of the House of Representatives, sessions of 1873–1876. Was elected State Senator in November, 1876, for a term of four years; re-elected November, 1880; elected president *pro tem.* for the extra session of 1883, and re-elected Senator November, 1884, and again November, 1888, for a term of four years. In January, 1885, he was again elected president *pro tem.* of the Senate for the session of 1885. At the end of his term he retired from public life, but he was not long permitted to enjoy agricultural pursuits, for at the State Republican Convention, June, 1894, he was nominated for Auditor General of Pennsylvania, and elected November 6 by a plurality of 239,278, the largest ever given since the office was created.

Mrs. Caroline Hepburn Powell, by her second marriage, has had issue (surname Mylin): Barbara Kendig, Helen and Mercy Anna.

> *viii. Edward Augustus,* b. December 5, 1849; studied medicine and graduated from the University of Pennsylvania in 1868, and d. at Fargo, North Dakota, September 6, 1887.

XXI. SUSAN HEPBURN,[3] (William,[2] Samuel,[1]) born in 1814, on her father's farm in Williamsport. At a camp meeting held in Lycoming County, in 1833, she experienced religion, and joined the M. E. Church. In 1840 she married Rev. G. L. Brown, and died May 5, 1841, at the house of her father-in-law, in Baltimore, leaving an infant daughter only three months old. Mrs. Brown was the eighteenth child and youngest daughter of Judge William Hepburn. She led a quiet and unobtrusive life, was noted for her piety, and died at the early age of twenty-seven years. Her infant daughter, named Anna Crecy Brown, was adopted by her uncle and aunt, Mr. Thomas P. and Crecy Hepburn Simmons, and by them reared. When her foster-parents died she went to reside with her cousin, Mrs. Charlotte Hepburn Simmons Slate, Williamsport, and there she remains.

George L. Brown was born in the city of Baltimore, January 16, 1809. He embraced religion in Frederick City, Md., in the winter of 1830, under the ministry of Rev. James Reed, of the Baltimore Conference; was received on trial by the same conference in the spring of 1833, and labored with acceptance and usefulness as an itinerant minister from the time he was admitted on trial until the spring of 1841, when he was compelled to yield to the force of disease, and take a supernumerary relation. In a short time he experienced a considerable improvement in his health and reported to Bishop Waugh that he was ready for active work. There being a vacancy on Lancaster circuit, Virginia, he was assigned to that charge sometime in June, 1841. In the month of March following he was reappointed to Lancaster circuit, where he was highly appreciated. Mr. Brown's talents as a preacher were of a useful order. He was a man of amiable spirit, of deep piety, and highly beloved in all his fields of labor. In the midst of his usefulness he was stricken with bilious fever, and after an illness of two weeks died September 24, 1842, in his 34th year, having survived his wife less than a year and a half. He was buried at White Marsh Church, Lancaster County, Virginia.

XXII. HUSTON HEPBURN,[3] (William,[2] Samuel,[1]) born August 17, 1817, in Williamsport; died April 4, 1891. He was the seventh son and nineteenth and youngest child of Judge William Hepburn. His mother (Elizabeth Huston), after whom he was named, was his father's second wife, and there were nine in the family—four sons and five daughters. He was a little over four years old when his father died, and ten when his mother passed away.

His opportunities for an education were only such as were afforded by the common subscription schools of that time. At the age of sixteen he was employed as a clerk in the store of his brother-in-law, Thomas P. Simmons, in the then village of Newberry—now a part of the city of Williamsport. Afterwards he served in the same capacity for Mr. Simmons in his store at Jersey Shore, whither he had removed, for about seven years. He then entered as a student in the law office of Hon. James Gamble, at that place, and was admitted to the Lycoming County bar in 1841. After remaining for a short time in the office of his preceptor, he was appointed deputy under Sheriff William Riddle, in the autumn of 1844, and served the entire term of three years.

In the spring of 1851 he entered into a law partnership with Mr. Gamble, at Jersey Shore, and for eighteen years it proved a most agreeable and pleasant association. During the service of Mr. Gamble in Congress (1851–1855) he managed the law business of the firm. In 1856, at the October election, Mr. Hepburn was chosen prothonotary of Lycoming County, and served the term of three years with satisfaction to the public.

December 9, 1856, he married Miss Susan, daughter of Charles McMicken, then a resident of Nippenose Township.

The fruits of this union were two daughters, when his wife died in 1863. On the 26th of March, 1868, he married, secondly, Miss Anna Simmons, niece of Thomas P. Simmons, a well remembered resident of Williamsport.

Early in the spring of 1870 Mr. Hepburn located on a farm in Nippenose Township, which was a part of the estate of the father of his first wife; but he was not permitted to long enjoy the life of an agriculturist. In the autumn of 1871 he was nominated by the Democratic party as a candidate for associate judge, and elected. He thus again became associated with his old preceptor and partner, who was then on the bench as president judge. In 1874 he permanently located in Williamsport, having received the appointment of deputy prothonotary. In 1880 he was reappointed to the same position. After serving to the end of the prothonotary's term, and when the weight of years was beginning to bear him down, he was appointed court crier, and performed the functions of that office almost to the close of his life.

It may be mentioned as a remarkable historical fact that Hon. William Hepburn was the *first* of the four associate judges appointed by Governor Mifflin on the passage of the bill erecting the county of Lycoming, April 13, 1795, and his son, Huston, was the *last* to sit upon the bench in that capacity, retiring in 1876, the Constitution of 1871–2 having abolished the office.

At the time of his death Judge Hepburn had been a member of the bar of Lycoming County for fifty years. He was thoroughly conversant with the law, but had practiced little for fifteen years preceding his death. He knew a great deal about the business of the county, however, and his services in this relation were often in demand. The day of his funeral (April 7, 1891,) the bar of Lycoming County met in the court house and took action on the death of their deceased member.

His remains were taken to Jersey Shore for interment in the cemetery at that place. A handsome monument marks his grave. His widow survives. There was no issue by the second marriage.

DESCENDANTS OF SAMUEL HEPBURN.

XXIII. HANNAH MARIA HEPBURN,[4] (Samuel,[3] James,[2] Samuel,[1]) born in Milton, Pa., December 25, 1812, eldest child of Samuel and Ann Clay Hepburn. She married William Henry Blackiston, of Kent County, Maryland, June 8, 1835, and took up her residence in that state, where she died in June, 1878. Mr. Blackiston was born near Sassafras, Md., October 2, 1813, and died in Middletown, Delaware, March 14, 1853. He was a farmer by occupation, owning and cultivating over 300 acres of land. They had issue (surname Blackiston):

> i. *Samuel Hepburn*, b. July 12, 1836, near Sassafras; m. Mrs. S. T. (Raisen) Brooks September 17, 1868, and d. October, 1883, leaving issue: Henry Curtis, Josephine, McCall, Helen and Slator Clay.
>
> ii. *Henry Curtis*, b. June 8, 1838 ; served as a lieutenant in Company B, 1st Maryland Cavalry (Confederate), and was killed in a skirmish at Bunker Hill, Va., September 3, 1864.
>
> iii. *Josephine*, b. November 5, 1839; m. Henry Augustus Nowland October 29, 1885, near Middletown, Delaware, who resides on a farm of 450 acres, which he owns; has been a member of the Legislature.
>
> iv. *Annie Jemima*, b. February 6, 1841 ; d. August 14, 1870.
>
> v. *Emma*, b. February 16, 1843, in Chestertown, Kent County, Maryland.
>
> vi. *Rev. Slator Clay*, b. January 13, 1846. Graduated at Nashotah Theological Seminary, Wisconsin; now rector of the Episcopal Church in Butte, Montana ; m. Margaret Monroe, of Missouri. Issue : Martha M., Annie I., Frances and Margaret.
>
> vii. *Clara Leete*, b. May 29, 1848; living in Middletown, Delaware.
>
> viii. *Lizzie*, b. October 18, 1849; m. Henry A. Nowland October 25, 1876 ; d. December 1, 1883, leaving issue (surname Nowland) : Maria Hepburn, Augustus James and Mary Blackiston.

DR. JAMES CURTIS HEPBURN,
Born 1815.

ix. Mary Eugenia, b. March 14, 1852; m., July 6, 1873, John Woodbridge Patton, of Philadelphia, son of Rev. John Patton and Mindwell Gould. Mr. Patton is a lawyer by profession, and practiced until about five years ago. He is now president of "The Mortgage Trust Company of Pennsylvania," Philadelphia. They have issue (surname Patton): John Woodbridge, Helen Hepburn, Agnes, Henry Blackiston and Mildred Gould.

XXIV. DR. JAMES CURTIS HEPBURN,[4] (Samuel,[3] James,[2] Samuel,[1]) born at Milton, Pa., March 13, 1815, son of Samuel and Ann Clay Hepburn. His mother was a daughter of Rev. Slator Clay and Hannah Hughes, widow of John Hughes, of Montgomery County, Pa. His grandfather, Slator Clay, was an Episcopal clergyman, rector of the church at Perkiomen, and the old Swede church near Norristown. Sketches of his ancestors on the paternal side have been given. His mother was an earnest Christian, fond of the Bible, exacting a strict observance of the Sabbath in her family, faithful in teaching the Catechism to her children, and inculcating truthfulness and good morals.

James Hepburn received his primary education in the Milton Academy under the celebrated Rev. David Kirkpatrick; graduated from Princeton in the fall of 1832, and united with the Presbyterian Church, Milton, in 1835. He studied medicine under Dr. Samuel Pollock, Milton, and received the degree of M. D. at the University of Pennsylvania in 1836, and that of LL. D. from Lafayette College in 1868. After graduation he practiced medicine for one year in West Philadelphia, and after that for a year at Norristown, Pa., when, becoming convinced that as a physician he was not needed in this country, where they abounded and were jostling one another, and that it was his duty to God and his fellow-men to go and labor in some other country where his talents would be more useful, was impelled to offer himself to the Presbyterian Board of Foreign Missions to go to any of the heathen nations to whom they would

be pleased to send him.   He was accordingly married to
Miss Clara Maria, daughter of Harvey Leete, Esq., of Fay-
etteville, N. C., on the 27th of October, 1840.   She was a
young lady in full sympathy with his views, and of an
earnest Christian and missionary spirit, whom he first met
while residing in Norristown.

Under the direction of the Board of Foreign Missions
they sailed on the 15th of March, 1841, from Boston in the
ship Potomac, Captain Carter, for Siam.   After a long and
trying voyage of one hundred and seven days, they arrived
at Batavia, island of Java, June 29th.   Here they remained
until the 7th of July, when they again set sail for Singapore, where they arrived on the 12th.   Their destination
being here changed for China, they remained in Singapore
about two years, studying the Malay and Chinese languages,
teaching a class of Chinese boys and prescribing for all the
sick that came to them.

After the so-called "Opium war" between England and
China was finished, and the five ports in China were opened
to foreign residents, they left Singapore and moved up to
China, landing at Macao in July, 1843 ; and in October they
went to Amoy, where they were stationed until the end of
1845.   Here, in conjunction with Dr. W. H. Cumming, Dr.
Hepburn opened a hospital for the Chinese, prescribing for
the sick, performing many surgical operations and teaching
the great truths of Christianity.

But their life in China was cut short by sickness, and
they were compelled to return to the home-land, landing in
New York in 1846, with one child.   Hoping to return to
China, they settled in New York and the Doctor went into
the practice of his profession.   Here they remained for
thirteen years, residing in Forty-second Street, then on the
outskirts of the city, working principally upon the lower
classes, until the spring of 1859, when Japan, being opened to
foreign trade and residence by the treaties of Commodore

Perry and Mr. Harris, and the Board of Foreign Missions calling for a physician to go there, Dr. Hepburn offered himself, broke up his home, and sailed for Japan in April, 1859. They landed at Yokohama on the 18th of October, having been detained in Shanghai some three weeks by sickness. With the exception of two missionaries who had come over from Shanghai a short time before them, Dr. Hepburn and his wife were the first missionaries to arrive in Japan after the country was opened.

It will be impossible within the limits of this sketch to give a detailed account of the life of Dr. Hepburn and his wife for thirty-three years in Japan, and of their work there. At first they had to endure many privations, and were exposed to many dangers, residing among people who were hostile to foreigners and to whom the name of Christian was synonymous with pernicious and corrupt religion, the followers of which were only to be arrested and punished with death. They were regarded with a great deal of suspicion and jealousy. Owing to this, as well as ignorance of the language, it was some three years before Dr. Hepburn could enter fully on his medical work or teaching the religion of Christ. Time, however, and kindly treatment of the people, and friendly intercourse, gradually dissolved their prejudices and brought them to regard the strangers as friends.

After opening his dispensary and hospital its fame soon spread and he had all the patients he could attend to, of every class of people and of every variety of disease ; besides many young men anxious to learn the practice of foreign medicine. The foreign system of medicine and surgery was quite unknown at that time in Japan, except by a very few who had obtained an imperfect knowledge of it from the Dutch of Nagasaki. Dr. Hepburn, therefore, was the first to perform any important surgical operations.

Along with his medical work and teaching the Bible, he

employed every spare moment to the study of the language, which, he says, is confessedly one of the most difficult of known languages. As the result of this study he compiled a Japanese and English dictionary, the *first* of the kind, and wrote a grammar of the Japanese language, and published them in Shanghai in 1867, as there were no facilities for publishing such works at that time in Japan. This dictionary has gone through three editions, being revised and greatly enlarged and improved each time, until it is now stereotyped and the only one of the kind still in use.

From the first the translation of the Bible into Japanese was a work which engaged his earnest attention as one of the most importance, being the basis and embodiment of all Christian teaching, and the only true source of enlightenment and civilization to the Japanese people. He worked at this alone with his Japanese teacher for several years, and had the manuscript copy of the New Testament done as far as the four gospels, and all the epistles, except Colossians, Acts and Revelations. In 1872 a committee of four persons, of whom he was one, was appointed by a convention of missionaries to devote themselves especially to this work. The revision of his work and translation was finished in 1878, and published on blocks. He was also on a committee of three to translate the Old Testament. This was finished, after some five years of work, in 1889.

Besides the above work he translated and published the *first* Christian Tract ever published in Japan; also the Shorter Catechism, Confession of Faith and some other Christian Tracts; also a Dictionary of the Bible of over 600 pages. Their last work in Japan was the erection of a very handsome brick church, capable of seating some 600 persons, for the native congregation with which he and his wife were specially identified. This was built from funds mainly collected from Christian people in this country.

Thus after thirty-three years of life and labor in Japan,

old age and increasing infirmities warned these two faithful missionaries that their work was done, and compelled them with much reluctance to seek rest and end their days in the land of their nativity.

During their long residence in Japan they won the confidence and respect of the natives with whom they came in contact, and their departure was a source of deep regret to their friends. It is hard to estimate the value of their great work in Japan in the introduction of Christianity, and in laying down and explaining the sublime truths of the gospel to a benighted people. After receiving unusual expressions of regard from cultivated Japanese, and from the missionaries with whom they had been associated in Christian labor, they left Tokio and arrived in San Francisco in November, 1892, where they were warmly welcomed by the good people of that city, who had known of their long and faithful work in the old Empire of the East. After passing the winter in Southern California, they wended their way east, and after visiting friends and the scenes of their youth, finally settled in East Orange, N. J., where, in the soft and mellow twilight of their well-spent lives, they calmly await the call of the Master to enter into a new and more glorious sphere.

Dr. James Curtis Hepburn and wife had issue :

i. *Samuel D.*, b. in Amoy, China, April 9, 1844; m. Miss Clara B. Shaw, of Lock Haven, Pa., October 16, 1873. They reside in Yokohama, Japan, where Mr. Hepburn is manager of a Japanese steamship company. They have no issue.

XXV. Sarah Hepburn,[4] (James,[3] Samuel,[2] Samuel,[1]) daughter of Samuel and Ann Clay Hepburn, born June 2, 1817, in Milton, Pa.; married James Pollock, of the same place, December 19, 1837, and died in Philadelphia August 24, 1886, in the 70th year of her age.

For one whose history is so well known it is unnecessary, in this connection, to speak in detail of the career of her distinguished husband. President judge, member of Congress, Governor of the state of Pennsylvania, and director of the Mint for many years, James Pollock was one of the most honored and respected citizens of the Commonwealth. In all his illustrious career there is perhaps no one incident of his busy life that shines with a more resplendent lustre, one that will live when political deeds are forgotten, than the fact that it was through his suggestion and influence that the sublime motto, "*In God We Trust*," was stamped on United States silver coins. He was then director of the Philadelphia Mint, and the great southern rebellion was at its height, when he made the suggestion to Secretary Chase of the United States Treasury, and it was at once adopted. It was a true Christian recognition of Divine power, an acknowledgment that those who put their faith in the God of battles cannot fail when right and justice are on their side.

Governor Pollock was born in Milton September 11, 1810, and died April 19, 1890, full of years and of honors, at the residence of his son-in-law, H. T. Harvey, Esq., of Lock Haven, Pennsylvania. James Pollock and Sarah Hepburn, his wife, had issue (surname Pollock):

> *i. Samuel H.*, d. October 25, 1865.
> *ii. William Curtis*, m. Ella M. Burr; live in Philadelphia.
> *iii. Louisa Annie*, m. Richard Edie Clay; live in Philadelphia.
> *iv. Emily Clara*, d. in infancy.
> *v. James Crawford*, m. Mary Angus Kelsey; live in Buffalo, N. Y.
> *vi. Sarah Margaret*, m. Henry Thomas Harvey, member of the bar, Lock Haven, Pa.
> *vii. Emma*, m. Charles Corss, member of the bar, Lock Haven, Pa.

XXVI. SLATOR CLAY HEPBURN,[4] (James,[3] Samuel,[2] Samuel,[1]) born October 19, 1819, at Milton, Pa., son of Samuel and Ann Clay Hepburn. He received an academical education at the Milton Academy under the Rev. David Kirkpatrick as principal. Entered Princeton College, New Jersey, and graduated therefrom in 1839; in 1844 he graduated from Princeton Theological Seminary. He was ordained to the gospel ministry by the Presbytery of Northumberland, January 21, 1845, and installed pastor of the Great Island Church (Lock Haven, Pa.,) the same day. That pastoral relation was dissolved June 11, 1850, and on the 2d of July following he was installed pastor of the Presbyterian Church of Hamptonburgh,* Orange County, New York, by the Presbytery of Hudson, and that pastorate still continues. It is rare to find an instance where the relation between pastor and people has existed for almost forty-four years; and in this case, particularly, it speaks volumes of praise in favor of both.

The Rev. Dr. Hepburn married, September 12, 1849, Anna Maria, daughter of Samuel and Anna Maria Boyd, of New York City. They have living issue:

> i. *Samuel Boyd*, b. February 6, 1854; m., October 24, 1882, Sarah, daughter of Alfred Booth, of Hamptonburgh, N. Y., and they have three children, viz.: Anna Bayard, Amy Lourie and Dolly Booth.

XXVII. MARY HEPBURN,[4] (James,[3] Samuel,[2] Samuel,[1]) fifth child and third daughter of Samuel and Ann Clay Hepburn, born May 1, 1822, in Milton, and resides in Lock Haven, Pa. She married Louis A. Mackey, a native of White Deer Township, Union County, Pa., where he was born November 25, 1819. When he was about ten years of age his parents removed to Milton, where he was placed in a school conducted upon the Lancasterian system, of which he soon became the principal " Monitor." At the age of twelve he was placed under the instruction of that famous educator, Rev. David Kirkpatrick, then in charge of the Milton Academy. He subsequently removed to Westmoreland County, but Mr. Mackey, with eight other young men,

---

*Post-office, Campbell Hall, N. Y.

followed him to his new home on the Loyalhanna and there completed their academic studies.

In 1835 he entered the junior class of Union College, Schenectady, and two years later graduated with the highest honors, the youngest of a class of 108. One year thereafter he commenced the study of law with Hon. James Pollock, of Milton, and after being under his instruction one year he entered the law school of Dickinson College, Carlisle, then conducted by Judge Read, and was admitted to the bar at Carlisle in 1840.

In February, 1841, he located in Lock Haven and engaged in the practice of law, which he continued with success until 1855, when he was chosen president of the Lock Haven Bank, and when it became a National Bank he was continued in the same relation.

Mr. Mackey was a delegate to the Whig National Convention in 1855, at Baltimore, and assisted in the nomination of General Scott for President. In 1872 he represented the XVIIIth Congressional District in the Democratic National Convention, held at Baltimore, and voted against the nomination of Horace Greeley. Four years before this (1868) he was the Democratic nominee for Congress in his district, but was defeated by Hon. William Hepburn Armstrong, of Williamsport. When Lock Haven became a city in 1870, he was elected its first mayor, and held the office for three years. Renominated again for Congress in 1874, he was elected, and re-elected in 1876 by a largely increased majority.

When Mr. Philip M. Price gave sixteen acres for the Central Normal School at Lock Haven, Mr. Mackey was the *first* man to subscribe $1,000 towards raising a fund to assist in erecting the buildings. At a meeting of the stockholders, held February 17, 1870, he was elected president of the board of trustees, and was re-elected for several successive terms.

Personally Mr. Mackey was a man of great popularity and numbered his friends by the hundreds. He was kind, obliging and hospitable. For years he was closely identified with the leading interests of his city and district, and he was characterized by quick discernment, sound judgment, liberality and enterprise. He took a leading interest in the construction of the Bald Eagle Valley Railroad, and for more than ten years served as its president. Mr. Mackey died suddenly of heart failure February 8, 1889, in the 70th year of his age, leaving a widow and two daughters to survive him. The eldest daughter, Annie H., married Dr. J. H. Hayes, and the youngest, M. Louise, married Dr. E. P. Ball. They all reside in Lock Haven.

DESCENDANTS OF ANDREW DOZ HEPBURN.

XXVIII. JAMES HUSTON HEPBURN,[4] (Andrew Doz,[3] James,[2] Samuel,[1]) born September 11, 1803; died July 30, 1853. Was the eldest son of Andrew Doz and Martha Huston Hepburn, and was born in Williamsport. He received a good education, and after studying law with Judge Thomson at Chambersburg, he was admitted to the bar of Franklin County. He located at Kittanning and began practice at that place. On the 1st of October, 1829, he was united in marriage with Mary McClellan, of Strasburg, Franklin County. Soon after they removed from Kittanning to Jersey Shore, Lycoming County, Pa., where Mr. Hepburn opened a retail dry goods store, which he carried on during the balance of his life, a period of about twenty-four years.

Mr. Hepburn was an active business man, and, aside from his mercantile pursuits, took a lively interest in whatever was calculated to develop the resources of the country. He was one of the organizers, and a director and treasurer of the Jersey Shore and Lewisburg Turnpike Company, subsequently known as the Jersey Shore Bridge Company. He was a man of more than ordinary ability and contrib-

uted many articles to agricultural papers. He was interested in farming and stock raising, and to him is due the
credit for having introduced Durham cattle in Lycoming
County. In politics he was a Whig and strongly adhered
to the principles of that party. He was a warm friend of
Henry Clay and deeply regretted his defeat for President.
True to the faith of his distinguished father and ancestors,
he was a Presbyterian and an ardent supporter of the Church.
Although dying at a comparatively early age, he was quite
successful in business and accumulated a comfortable competence. After his decease his wife, who was a careful,
methodical business woman, carried on the store till near
her death, which occurred January 26, 1873. They had
issue :

> *i. George M.*, b. July 8, 1830; d. June 16, 1855.
>
> *ii. Andrew D.*, b. February 27, 1832 ; d. April 5, 1834.
>
> *iii. McClellan Patterson*, b. July 31, 1835; studied dentistry and
> practiced for two years in Williamsport ; m. Miss Nancy Eleanor
> Hays May 3, 1859, and settled on a farm near Pine Creek, part
> of which was owned by his great-grandfather (James Hepburn)
> one hundred years ago. He is the owner of a unique writing
> desk, of the colonial period, containing a secret drawer, which
> once belonged to Thomas Huston, his maternal grandfather.
> Issue: 1. M. Hays. 2. James Huston. He graduated from
> Jefferson Medical College April, 1886. Afterwards studied in
> Vienna and other European schools. Is now practicing in
> Washington, D. C. 3. William M. 4. Mary McClellan.
>
> *iv. Martha*, b. September 24, 1837 ; d. January 31, 1855.
>
> *v. Lydia*, b. ———, 1839 ; m. Dr. Benjamin Bear; d. June 2, 1894.
> Issue: One son and one daughter, William M. and Mary M.
> Bear.

It may be mentioned as a strange coincidence that her
funeral took place at 2:30 p. m., June 5, 1894, the day being
the 34th anniversary of her marriage, which occurred at the
same hour, in the same house, and Rev. Dr. Joseph Stevens,
who officiated on that occasion, preached her funeral
sermon.

JUDGE SAMUEL HEPBURN,
Born 1806.

XXIX. SAMUEL HEPBURN,[4] (Andrew Doz,[3] James,[2] Samuel,[1]) second son of Andrew Doz and Martha Huston Hepburn, born November 26, 1806, in Williamsport; married
at Silver's Spring, Cumberland County, Pa., October 20,
1829, Rebecca, daughter of David Williamson. She was
born October 1, 1807, near Newville, Cumberland County,
and died near Carlisle August 31, 1892. Her ancestors
were all Scots and came from Fief, Scotland, and in early
colonial times settled in Cumberland Valley, Pennsylvania.
Her maternal great-grandfather, John McKnight, served as
captain in the French and Indian war, and was under General Forbes at the capture of Fort Du Quesne.

Samuel Hepburn commenced reading law under the direction of Hon. James Armstrong, his uncle, at Williamsport, and completed his last year of study in Judge Read's
law school connected with Dickinson College. He was
admitted to the bar in Carlisle in 1835. Just after his admission he was appointed by Judge Read Professor of Law
in Dickinson College. He was admitted to practice in the
Supreme Court of the United States on motion of Hon.
James Buchanan, afterwards President of the United States,
in 1838.

Having married in Cumberland County, he settled permanently in Carlisle, and after retiring from his professor-
ship in the law school, he at once entered upon the practice
of his chosen profession. Being apt, studious and industrious, he soon built up a good practice and established for
himself an excellent reputation at the bar. One of the elements of his success was a remarkably retentive memory,
which often aided him very materially in the trial of
an important cause.

He was appointed president judge of the IXth Judicial
District February 2, 1839, for a period of ten years, by Gov.
David R. Porter. By an act of the Legislature, passed
March 9, 1847, the common pleas business of Dauphin

County was given to Judge Hepburn, and, by an arrangement with Judge Eldred, of the Dauphin district, Judge Hepburn took the civil list cases, and Judge Eldred the criminal cases.

"Judge Hepburn," says the History of the Susquehanna and Juniata Valleys (pp. 681–1200), "was held in high estimation by the members of the bar of the counties where he held courts. When he held his last court in Dauphin County, at the expiration of his ten years, the bar met, passed and forwarded to Judge Hepburn most complimentary resolutions, which they had unanimously adopted. Some one in Juniata, who knew him well when on the bench, said he was young, handsome and brilliant. He was quite a young man when he went upon the bench, and in the very vigor of manhood he resumed the practice of his profession. * * * As a judge he was rapid, accurate and clear in the trial of causes, and his career as a judge was highly creditable to himself and satisfactory to the people of the district."

In 1848 the degree of LL. D. was conferred on him by Jefferson College. His commission as president judge having expired, he was succeeded in 1849 by Judge Watts, who was appointed by Governor Johnson for the term of ten years, but under the amended Constitution judges were made elective by the people in 1851, so that Judge Watts' term was cut off in December, 1851.

On his retirement from the bench Judge Hepburn resumed the practice of law. Some years later Hon. Frederick T. Frelinghuysen, who afterwards became Secretary of State under President Arthur, and Judge Hepburn became the counsel who organized the Delaware Division Canal Company, Mr. Frelinghuysen acting for the New Jersey stockholders and Judge Hepburn for the Pennsylvania stockholders. Whilst serving in this capacity he remained some years in Philadelphia, where he had a large practice,

ːn returned to Carlisle and resumed business there,
he has continued without interruption. And to-day
ne of the oldest practitioners in the state. His career
ɔar has been brilliant and successful. In the beauti-
n of Carlisle, where he has lived so many years, he
ːides, after a long and busy life, "in a green old age,
ılly watching the lengthening shadows."
ːe Samuel Hepburn and wife had issue :

ː. *Andrew Doz*, b. November 14, 1830, in Williamsport; m. Henrietta McGuffy, at University of Virginia, 1857.
ːi. *John Williamson*, d. in infancy.
ːi. *William Williamson*, b. June 20, 1834. After completing his
preparatory studies at Carlisle, he entered the University of Virginia, and afterwards Princeton College. On leaving college he
commenced business as a partner in a wholesale merchant firm in
Philadelphia. A few years after he returned to Carlisle, where he
was chosen cashier of the First National Bank. His health, never
very vigorous, soon began to fail rapidly, and he d. January 26,
1864. Mr. Hepburn was a man of exceedingly attractive character.
To his fine intellectual accomplishments were added the graces
of great amiability of disposition, inflexible integrity and truthfulness, and sincere, unobtrusive piety.
ːv. *Martha Huston*, d. in infancy.
ːv. *Charles Huston*, b. November 1, 1837; d. August 13, 1892.
ːi. *Samuel*, b. December 30, 1839; m., first, Maria Moore; secondly,
Marie Japy; d. March 28, 1890.
ːi. *Anna*, b. January 5, 1842; m. William M. Watts November 26,
1872; resides in Carlisle.
ːi. *Hopewell*, b. January 4, 1844; now living in Carlisle. Not married.
ː. *Alexander McGill*, b. March 7, 1846; d. prematurely at the age
of 22. He had gone to his new home, Ingleside, Westmoreland County, Virginia, and was just entering on what promised
to be a happy and useful life, when he fell a victim to typhoid
fever, and d. September 20, 1868.
ː. *Henry Martyn*, b. October 21, 1851; living in Carlisle; has been
for some years the borough engineer. Not married.

ː. JANET HEPBURN,[4] (Andrew Doz,[3] James,[2] Sam-
ːe fourth child and second daughter of Andrew Doz
ırtha Huston Hepburn, born in Williamsport March

29, 1808, married Baker Langcake and settled near M
Pa.

Mr. Langcake was a native of Frankford, near Ph
phia, where he was born January 23, 1803. In 18
moved to Williamsport, where he met Janet Hepburn,
he married September 18, 1829. He was a man '
judgment was ripened by long experience in busines
1839 he located in Muncy, where he engaged in the
cantile business, which he conducted for many years
was identified with many interests of the town and
much pleasure in its prosperity. He was among th
to encourage the project of a cemetery and subs
largely of stock for that purpose. It is now one
most beautiful burial places in the West Branch V
adorned with chaste and appropriate tributes to the
one of the most beautiful and imposing of which i
cenotaph erected to perpetuate the name, fame and he
of Capt. John Brady, Revolutionary soldier and defen
the infant settlement, who perished at the hands
savages on his return from Fort Muncy April 11, 177

Mr. Langcake, throughout his long life, was noted f
high integrity, love of truth and devotion to duty. In
ious belief he was a Presbyterian. His death occurred
28, 1893, at the mature age of 90 years, 3 months and 5
For sixty-four years he and his wife had traveled life's
together, and during that time death had never invade
family until he himself was called. At this writing
cember 1, 1894,) his venerable widow still survives, h
entered upon her 87th year. They had issue (sur
Langcake):

       i. Martha Hepburn, m. Capt. John M. Bowman, of Muncy.
          have one son, Baker Langcake Bowman, and he is Janet
          grandson.
       ii. J. Augustus; single.
       iii. Sarah Elizabeth, m. Dr. Robert Hayes Seiler.

XXXI. DR. WILLIAM HEPBURN,[4] (Andrew Doz,[3] James,[2] Samuel,[1]) born December 29, 1812, in Williamsport, Pa.; married Elizabeth Irvine, of Cumberland County, and died October 5, 1855.

He received his preparatory education principally in his native town, after which he read medicine under the direction of Dr. James Rankin, of Muncy, and graduated in 1835. Soon afterwards he located at Mill Hall, Clinton County, Pa., where he followed his profession for eighteen months, when he removed to Jersey Shore, Pa., in 1838. There Dr. Hepburn practiced his profession for eleven years. Becoming dissatisfied with the practice of medicine, he went to Carlisle in 1850, studied law with his brother, Hon. Samuel Hepburn, and was admitted to the bar. His health failing soon afterwards, he returned to Williamsport, where he died as stated above.

Miss Elizabeth Irvine, whom Dr. Hepburn married May 23, 1837, was born November 13, 1816. Her grandfather, James Irvine, was of Scotch-Irish descent, born in the North of Ireland, and came to this country at an early day. Her grandmother was Sarah Harris, a relative of the early Harris family of Bellefonte. Her father, John Irvine, was the eldest son of James and Sarah Harris Irvine. He married Eliza Lamberton, and she became the mother of Mrs. Dr. William (Elizabeth) Hepburn.

Dr. William Hepburn and wife had issue:

> i. *Martha Jane*, b. April 15, 1838; m. Hon. Henry C. Parsons, of Williamsport, October 17, 1865.
>
> ii. *William Irvine*, b. August 12, 1840. He is engaged as a real estate operator in Sioux City, Iowa, and in Wisconsin. Unmarried.
>
> iii. *Charles Walker*, b. March 25, 1843. He is married and resides in Iowa.
>
> iv. *Sarah Harris*, unmarried; resides with her mother in Williamsport.

> *v. Elizabeth*, m. Cyrus K. Small September 2, 1874; resides in New
>   York City.
> *vi. Mary*, m. Garret D. Tinsman November 24, 1872; resides in
>   Williamsport.

HON. HENRY C. PARSONS, a sketch of whose parents has already been given, was born in the borough of Jersey Shore, February 10, 1834. He removed with his parents to Williamsport when a few months old and has resided here to the present time. When of sufficient age he was prepared for college in the schools of his adopted city, and in 1851 he entered the Sophomore class of Brown University, Providence, Rhode Island, from which he was graduated in 1854. His tastes and opportunities led him to embrace the profession of the law, and after a thorough course of study in the office of his father, then practicing in Philadelphia, he was admitted to the bar in 1857. Returning to his native county in the fall of that year, he opened a law office in Williamsport, and has since practiced there, and attained prominence as one of the ablest lawyers of Pennsylvania.

In 1861 Mr. Parsons enlisted and served as sergeant of Company A, Eleventh Pennsylvania Volunteers, and in 1864 he made a second campaign as captain of Company B, One Hundred and Fifteenth Pennsylvania Volunteers.

He was elected a member of the Constitutional Convention of 1873–74, to revise the Constitution of the state, an honor he shared with the most distinguished talent of that body.

Mr. Parsons was elected mayor of Williamsport in 1881, and his administration, covering the years 1882 and 1883, was marked by business-like conduct of the city's affairs. When he left the chief magistracy of the city he carried with him the thanks and best wishes of his fellow-citizens irrespective of party. Since 1882 he has served as president of the West Branch National Bank, of Williamsport, the oldest banking house in the city, and is vice-president of the Savings Institution of the same city. Mr. Parsons is a Republican, and belongs to Reno Post, G. A. R., of Williamsport. He is in the full prime and vigor of manhood and is still actively engaged in the practice of his profession.

As stated before, Mr. Parsons married Miss Martha J. Hepburn, and they have had issue (surname Parsons): 1. Elizabeth Hepburn. 2. Frank, married Miss Elizabeth Watson October 10, 1894. 3. John R. 4. Hepburn. 5. Harry.

ANCESTRY OF THE PARSONS FAMILY.

The following, contributed by the Rev. Horace Edwin Hayden, of Wilkes-Barre, Pa., was received after the foregoing had been printed:

Cornet Joseph Parsons, of Great Torrington, England, came to Massachusetts with Hon. William Pynchon, and with him settled Springfield, Massachusetts, in 1636. In 1655 he left Springfield and was a principal founder of Northampton, Massachusetts, where he engaged in the fur trade and became a very wealthy man. He declined all offices except that of Selectman, which he held for years, and that of Cornet, which he received in 1678. The title of Cornet was of much more importance then than now. He died October 9, 1683. He married, November 26, 1646, at Springfield, Mary, daughter of Thomas Bliss. By her he had eleven children, of whom three died single. His eldest son, Hon. Joseph Parsons, was ancestor of Hon. Levi Parsons Morton, ex-Vice-President of the United States, and now Republican Governor-elect (December 1, 1894,) of New York, and a number of eminent clergymen, physicians and lawyers, among whom my father, Hon Edwin Parsons Hayden, was not the least.

Samuel Parsons, the fourth son of Cornet Parsons, born January 23, 1652, married, first, about 1677, Elizabeth, daughter of Capt. Aaron Cook. She died September 2, 1690. He married, second, 1691, Rhoda, born September 26, 1669, daughter of John and Thankful Woodward Taylor.

He married, third, December 15, 1711, Mary Wheeler. He had—

1. Samuel, b. 1678; d. 1679.
2. Samuel, b. 1680; d. 1683.
3. Eliza, b. 1684.
4. Jemima, b. 1691.
5. Rhoda, b. 1694.
6. Timothy, b. 1696; had three sons.
7. Hannah, b. 1699.
8. Simeon, b. 1701; had three sons.
9. Phineas, b. 1704.
10. Aaron, b.——.
11. Ithamar, b. Durham, Connecticut, 1707, his father having moved there in 1706. He d. January 21, 1786. He had David, Nathan, Rhoda, Sarah, Ithamar, of Whitestone, N. Y., Naomi, and Aaron.

David, the eldest, settled at Granville, Massachusetts, and had Col. Seth Parsons, of Granville, and Joel Parsons, the father of Hon. Anson V. Parsons, and of Mrs. Eliza Miner, of Litchfield, and of Sophronia, Rachel Dennis and Eleanora Parsons.

Wilkes-Barre, Pa.   HORACE EDWIN HAYDEN.

XXXII. DR. ANDREW HEPBURN,[4] (Andrew Doz,[3] James,[2] Samuel,[1]) son of Andrew Doz and Martha Huston Hepburn, was born in Williamsport, Pa., December 15, 1814. His education began in the schools and academy of his native town and was completed at Dickinson College, Carlisle. After his graduation he commenced reading medicine under the direction of his brother, Dr. William Hepburn, who was then following his profession in Mill Hall, Clinton County, Pa. He entered Jefferson Medical College, Philadelphia, in 1840, and, taking a full course, graduated in the spring of 1841.

Dr. Andrew Hepburn married Miss Elizabeth Sharon McMeen in 1843. She belonged to the well-known family of that name which settled on the river just west of Williams-

DR. ANDREW HEPBURN,
Born 1814.
Died 1872.

port, soon after the close of the Revolutionary war, and was a daughter of Col. John McMeen.

Soon after their marriage they emigrated to Ohio and settled at Bellevue. In a short time they removed to Tiffin, as Dr. Hepburn believed that that place would be better for his profession. Here he remained until 1851. During this time he was actively employed and built up a large practice. During the cholera epidemic in Tiffin the exactions of his profession were so unremitting that he overtaxed his strength and took the " chills and fever," which impaired his health. Soon after this he was requested to come to Williamsport by his father, as he and his wife were getting old, and she was too feeble to keep house. Dr. Hepburn yielded to the solicitations of his parents, broke up his home at Tiffin and returned to Williamsport. His mother died February 6, 1852, not long after his return. At Tiffin Dr. Hepburn was held in such high esteem by the people that they were loth to see him depart.

At the call for surgeons after the first battle of Bull Run, Dr. Hepburn promptly responded, notwithstanding his shattered health, and repaired to Washington. But owing to his physical condition he necessarily remained but a short time.

Dr. Hepburn continued to make Williamsport his home until his death, which occurred June 10, 1872. His wife died in June, 1882. They resided in the old homestead on the north side of the public square and Market Street. He was true to the faith of his fathers and died a staunch Presbyterian, having succeeded his father as elder and superintendent of the Sunday school in the First Presbyterian Church, Williamsport. Dr. Hepburn enjoyed a wide acquaintance ; was noted for his kindness of heart, purity and high integrity of character. As a business man he was conservative and cautious. He inherited considerable real estate from his father, and was one of the executors of his large estate. His own will (see Book B, p. 524,) is carefully drawn and liberal provision made for his children.

Dr. Andrew Hepburn and his wife Elizabeth had issue:

>   *i. Andrew Doz*, b. December 23, 1844; unmarried; is a resident of Philadelphia.
>
>   *ii. Clara Elizabeth*, b. August 14, 1847; unmarried; resides in Freehold, N. J.
>
> 37. *iii. Robert Hopewell*, b. July 2, 1850; m. Miss Elizabeth Hunt, of Catasaqua, Pa., October 3, 1877; resides in Avondale, Chester County, Pa.
>
>   *iv. William McMeen*, b. June 5, 1855; m. Miss Sarah E. Green, of Long Branch, N. J., June 2, 1886. Studied medicine and is a practicing physician in Freehold, N. J. He is an elder and superintendent of the Sunday school of the First Presbyterian Church in that place, following the example of his great-grandfather James, his grandfather Andrew Doz, and his father, Dr. Andrew Hepburn.

XXXIII. THOMAS HEPBURN,[4] (Andrew Doz,[3] James,[2] Samuel,[1]) born in Williamsport ——————, and died August 8, 1873, in Baltimore. He was raised in Williamsport and when of sufficient age engaged in agricultural pursuits on one of his father's farms near the city. On the 27th of December, 1842, he married Miss Mary Scudder, of Trenton, New Jersey, and they settled in Williamsport, in a brick house standing on East Third Street, which was built by Michael Ross, the founder of Williamsport, about the close of the last century. Having become associated with the Northern Central Railroad Company, Mr. Hepburn removed to Baltimore to take charge of a branch of their business in that city. And there he continued to reside until the time of his death as already stated. His wife survived him till the 20th of January, 1884, when she died. They had issue:

>   *i. Andrew Doz*, b.——, 1843. He m. Martha P. Fowler, of Calvert County, Maryland, in 1862, and she d. in 1871. No issue. Mr. Hepburn d. in August, 1880.

ii. Charles H., b. July 14, 1845; m. Laura F., fourth daughter of Colonel Edwin and Hannah Megready Wilmer, March 26, 1874. Issue: 1. Florence Wilmer, b. December 30, 1881. 2. Janette Small, b. September 19, 1883. 3. Alice Blanche, b. May 26, 1885; d. in infancy. The family resides in Baltimore. Mr. Hepburn is agent for the Erie and Western Transportation Company, Anchor Line, by lake and rail.

iii. Janette* Scudder (twin with Charles), b. July 14, 1845; m. Edward C., son of Henry and Eliza Small, of Limington, Maine, in 1864, and he d. April 27, 1876. Issue: 1. Edward C., now a mining engineer, Denver, Colorado. 2. Ralph D., lawyer in Chicago. 3. James D., student at Princeton, N. J. Mrs. Small resides at Hotel Thorndike, Jamestown, R. I.

DESCENDANTS OF JUDGE HEPBURN, OF CARLISLE.

XXXIV. ANDREW D. HEPBURN,[5] D. D., LL. D., (Samuel,[4] Andrew Doz,[3] James,[2] Samuel,[1]) eldest son of Samuel and Rebecca Williamson Hepburn, was born in Williamsport, Pa., November 14, 1830. His parents removed to Carlisle, Pa., in 1834. Here he pursued his preparatory studies and completed the Freshman year at Dickinson College. In 1848 he entered the Sophomore class of Jefferson College, Canonsburg, Pa., and was graduated in 1851. After spending two years at the University of Virginia, he entered the Theological Seminary at Princeton, and having completed the full course of study was graduated in 1857. In the same year he was licensed to preach by the Presbytery of Carlisle, and on October 22, 1858, was ordained by the Presbytery of Lexington, Virginia. His first and only pastoral charge was that of New Providence Church in Rockbridge County, Virginia. In 1859 he was elected professor of mental philosophy and rhetoric in the University of North Carolina, where he remained until 1867. Having obtained leave of absence, he spent one year of this period in

---

*It will be observed that this is the first departure from the spelling of "Janet," which had been in vogue in the family from early Scottish times up to 1845. And so far as known, Mrs. Small is the youngest member of the Hepburn family bearing the historic name.

Germany, at the University of Berlin. In 1868 he was elected professor of logic and English literature at Miami University, Oxford, Ohio, and in 1871 was chosen president of that University. In 1874 he was elected professor of mental philosophy in Davidson College, North Carolina, and in 1877 became president. He returned to Miami University as professor of rhetoric and English literature in 1885, and still holds that position. He is the author of a Manual of Rhetoric, published in 1874.

He was married July 10, 1857, to Henrietta, daughter of William H. McGuffey, D. D., LL D., of the University of Virginia. His two children are Charles McGuffey Hepburn and Henrietta Williamson Hepburn.

CHARLES McGUFFEY, son of Andrew D. and Henrietta McGuffey Hepburn, was born in Brownsburg, Rockbridge County, Virginia, on August 19, 1858. Most of his childhood was passed at Chapel Hill, North Carolina. In 1868 his parents removed to Oxford, Ohio. He there attended the public schools. In the fall of 1871 he entered the preparatory department of Miami University, and had completed its course and some of the work of the Freshman class, when the university closed in the summer of 1873.

In the autumn of 1874 he entered the Freshman class of Davidson College, from which he was graduated as A. B., valedictorian, and medalist of the Philanthropic Literary Society, in 1878. The two following years were passed at the University of Virginia, where he received the degree of Bachelor of Law in 1880. During the succeeding college year he had charge of the preparatory classes in Davidson College. In 1881 he was admitted to practice by the Supreme Court of Ohio. His office has been from the first in Cincinnati; his practice has been exclusively civil. A legal treatise by him on the theory and practice of code pleading in the statement of a cause of action is announced as in preparation.

He is one of the early members of the Ohio Club and of the Young Men's Democratic Club, both of Cincinnati, and has long been corresponding secretary of the former organization. For some years he has been one of the trustees of the Beta Tuela Pi Fraternity.

Mr. Hepburn was married on October 10, 1891, to Miss Julia Benedict, youngest daughter of the late Rev. Samuel Benedict, D. D., long rector of St. Paul P. E. Church, Cincinnati. There are two children of this marriage, Samuel Benedict Hepburn, born August 9, 1892, and Henrietta Hepburn, born February 5, 1894. Mr. and Mrs. Hepburn reside at Avondale, one of the suburbs of Cincinnati.

XXXV. Dr. Charles Huston Hepburn,[5] (Samuel,[4] Andrew Doz,[3] James,[2] Samuel,[1]) son of Samuel and Rebecca Williamson Hepburn, born November 1, 1837, at Carlisle; died August 13, 1892, suddenly, of apoplexy, while seated in a chair in his office.

After graduating from Dickinson College he entered the University of Virginia, where he remained for a short time and then went to Europe to pursue his studies in the University of Heidelberg. He was then a young man of twenty-two, and was appointed vice-consul at Antwerp, Belgium. His main purpose, however, was to have the range of European institutions of learning. He spent much time afterwards at Munich and Dresden.

Upon his return home he took up the study of law, graduated at Harvard Law School, and was admitted to the bar of Cumberland County in April, 1863. He practiced for a short time, but his characteristic modesty made the contentions of legal life distasteful to him, and he soon abandoned it for the reason that he did not care to present a case in court. He then served for some years as cashier of the First National Bank, Carlisle, when he turned his attention to the study of medicine and graduated from Jefferson Medical College.   He also spent some time in his earlier years in the Academy of Design, New York City.

Soon after the founding of the Indian Training School at Carlisle, he was appointed as physician to the school, although the benefit of his knowledge of education and educational institutions was one of the objects.   After spending some time in that capacity he was made chief clerk, which position he held until his death, and in which he served the institution to good advantage.   He was a member of the commission which settled the Indian difficulties in the Sioux country several years ago.

In 1883 he was elected a member of the Carlisle School Board and served in that capacity until his death.   He was president of the board for some years, and was re-elected within a few months of his decease.

Personally he was of a retiring disposition and his aversion to anything like notoriety was so great as to prove a barrier in the way of advancement to positions for which he was eminently fitted; and only in recent years such persons as were closely associated with him were aware of his remarkable attainments.   He was not only scholarly but brilliant, and with all his study seemed to forget nothing.   He had qualities which would have insured success in any profession, yet he followed none.   He was a fine conversationalist, full of anecdote and reminiscence, and by his urbane and pleasing manners drew around him many admiring friends. As a member of the school board his varied attainments were apparent, yet he always avoided the public duties it entailed. Even at the last commencement, after having done a greater part of the preliminary work, he refused to preside on Commencement Day.

At his funeral the school board attended in a body.   The pall-bearers were Congressman F. E. Beltzhoover, Joseph Bosler, A. J. Standing, Dr. J. R. Bixler, W. A. Hipple and R. P. Henderson.   The services were conducted by Rev. Mc-

SAMUEL HEPBURN, JR.
BORN 1839   DIED 1890

Millan, of the Episcopal Church, and his remains were laid at rest in the Old Graveyard.   Dr. Hepburn never married.

XXXVI. Samuel Hepburn, Jr.,[5] (Samuel,[4] Andrew D.,[3] James,[2] Samuel,[1]) born December 30, 1839, at Carlisle, Pa , son of Samuel and Rebecca Williamson Hepburn, died at sea on board the steamer Iroquois, off Charleston, S. C., March 28, 1890. Mr. Hepburn, accompanied by his son Charles, had gone to New York to take the steamer for Florida. He had been in bad health for some time and it was thought a sea voyage and sojourn in Florida would be beneficial. When near Charleston he had a recurrence of heart trouble, and on the 28th of March he died, suddenly, of apoplexy. His remains were brought home from Charleston and buried in Ashland Cemetery, Carlisle.

As remarked by one of his contemporaries, Mr. Hepburn entered the Carlisle bar well equipped by education, training, heredity and mode of thought, for the high duties of his office. After passing through the public schools of his native town and entering Dickinson College, and later the University of Virginia, he went to Europe, where he was connected with the Consulate at Antwerp under the U. S Consul, Hon. J. W. Quiggle, for some time, which gave him an excellent opportunity to pursue his studies abroad. He afterwards spent considerable time in the Universities of Berlin and Heidelberg; and before his return home he traveled extensively in southern Europe. The facility with which he acquired a foreign language was remarkable ; he was a thorough French, German and Italian scholar, conversing with ease in any of these languages, and this knowledge was invaluable to him in his profession.

The *Carlisle Volunteer*, under date of April 2, 1890, pays him this handsome tribute:

Samuel Hepburn, Jr., was the son of ex-Judge Samuel Hepburn. He entered Dickinson College but did not graduate. He then entered the University of Virginia, and later went to Europe and entered the University of Berlin. Returning home, he read law with his father and was admitted to the Carlisle bar. His great legal ability was soon recognized and brought to him the most lucrative practice at the bar. This he easily held. But his reputation as a lawyer was not simply local. His ability was recognized before the Supreme Court, and his practice before that court embraced the most important of the Cumberland County appeals.

He was a great lawyer. Coupled with a thorough knowledge of all the intricacies of the law, he had the faculty of grasping a subject in its entirety, selecting the salient points and then presenting them with a clearness and force that was most convincing to court and jury. It is no difficult matter to recall instances when others faltered, he, farther-sighted, presented some new feature of the case—usually a point of law—that won the verdict. He was an original thinker, clear and correct, and this, together with his frankness of statement and honesty of purpose, gave his opinions weight. A leading characteristic of the man was his wonderful retentive faculty. He could go through the most intricate case and pile up testimony, and yet so clear would be his recollection that he could correct the slightest contradiction in testimony, and an appeal to the stenographer's notes almost invariably substantiated his claims. A firm friend or a bitter enemy—there was no treachery in his make-up, and even his antagonisms gained for him respect.

At a meeting of the bar, previous to the funeral, eulogistic addresses were made by a number of members, when Mr. Weakley presented the following resolutions:

Samuel Hepburn, Jr., for more than twenty-five years an attorney and counselor of the Cumberland County Bar; a man conspicuous for his attractions in appearance and manner; gifted with unusual mental endowments; courteous in his professional and social intercourse with all men; a gentleman of liberal education, whose acquaintance was prized by men of professional and social eminence throughout the state; a carefully trained lawyer who brought to his professional career ripe scholarship and wide knowledge of the world; who devoted himself entirely to his profession and won in it with ease an honorable and conspicuous rank; who always displayed a chivalric devotion to the interest of his clients; whose forensic efforts before the court and jury, through a long and brilliant career, won the admiration of rivals as of friends; whose liberality and benevolence of thought and act were spontaneous and unceasing; who commanded without effort, and held with a firm grasp, a wide and growing circle of friends; whose strength grew rapidly with his years and who even in defeat increased his professional reputation with every contest; in the maturity of his manhood, with the fairest promise that his bright career would continue to the full measure of human life, has been suddenly called from earth.

That his memory may be preserved for the profession which he loved, and that it may be known that we appreciate his labors, his learning, his gentleness of character, his brilliant achievements, we write on the record of the court:

That we deplore his untimely end.

That we recognize in sorrow that we have been deprived of the stimulus of his professional power.

That for ourselves we mourn the loss of one whose generous courtesy claimed our constant esteem and friendship, and for the community the loss of one of its brightest, most generous and most conspicuous members.

That we tender to his bereaved family our condolence for their irreparable loss, and the assurance that the esteem and friendship we now express for him will extend to them as long as memory lasts.

This magnificent tribute was signed by J. M. Weakley, C. P. Humrich, John Hays, J. W. Wetzel and E. W. Biddle. Remarks were then made by members of the committee, touching on their personal and business relations with him, and speaking in the highest terms of his recognized ability and the loss his death would be to the community. Mr. Graham, of West Pennsboro, said the news of his death created in the rural districts an impression similar to that caused by the death of Lincoln and Garfield. The bar then adjourned and attended the funeral in a body.

The following memorial, written by Louis W. Hall, Esq., is taken from the Harrisburg *Patriot*, of April 1, 1890:

Samuel Hepburn, Jr., was one of the best of Pennsylvania's lawyers,—indeed, he would have ranked one of the foremost of any bar in or out of the state. As an all-round lawyer he had few equals and no superiors. He was able, forcible and lucid. In perception he was strong and clear. In style, ornate without being either incipid or meretricious. Free from pedantry and unpleasant affectation, he showed that he was master of his subject, having the ability to express his ideas in choicest English and fewest words. A born lawyer, he was both brilliant and clever, stating the real point of a case and confining his argument to it.

Samuel Hepburn, Jr., was endowed with a wonderful intellect. Had he lived and practiced law in New York, Philadelphia or Chicago instead of Carlisle, where opportunities would have drawn him out, he would have been regarded as one of the best lawyers of the land. Handsome, accomplished, talented, generous, his death will be an irreparable loss to the bar of the state.

No higher tribute need be added than has already been paid him in the above extracts from the notices of his death contained in the leading publications of his section of the state, and the contributions from his brother members of the bar.

Samuel Hepburn, Jr., married, first, Maria Parker Moore, by whom he had two children, viz.:

    i. Maria Moore, b. December, 1865; d. February, 1869.

    ii. Samuel Moore, b. March, 1867; now a civil engineer.

Mrs. Hepburn died in 1870, when Samuel Hepburn, Jr., married, second, Marie Japy, by whom he had six children, viz.:

    i. Charles Japy, b. September, 1872; now pursuing the study of law in Washington, D. C.

    ii. William Williamson, b. November, 1873; now at Avondale, Pa.

    iii. Louis Frederic, b. January, 1875.

    iv. Arthur Japy, b. October, 1877; entered U. S. Naval Academy, Annapolis, Md., in 1893.

ROBERT HOPEWELL HEPBURN

BORN 1850

v. Marie Louise, b. August, 1879.
vi. Donald McKnight, b. June, 1881.

DESCENDANT OF DR. ANDREW HEPBURN.

XXXVII.   ROBERT HOPEWELL HEPBURN,[5] (Andrew,[4] Andrew D.,[3] James,[2] Samuel,[1]) born July 2, 1850, at Tiffin, Ohio, son of Andrew and Elizabeth McMeen Hepburn, being named after Capt. Robert Ritchie of Revolutionary fame, one of his great-grandfathers on his mother's side, and Judge Hopewell Hepburn, of Pittsburg, his great-uncle (Hopewell being the family name of the Judge's mother), came to Williamsport with his parents when a year old, where he remained until he grew up, making it practically his native city.

He was a member of the class of 1871 of Princeton College, also of the well known "Whig" Literary Society and the Fraternity of Zeta Psi of that University.   He is Past Eminent Commander of the Knights Templar, Past High Priest of the Royal Arch Masons, Past Master Blue Lodge Masons and a Thirty-second Degree Mason.

When emergency men were called out in 1863 during the invasion of Pennsylvania by the rebels, and just previous to the battle of Gettysburg, he surreptitiously left home with them, attaching himself to Company B, Fourth Regiment; not being quite 15 years of age he could not be enrolled among the members.   He participated in the riots of 1877 as a private, until the attack upon the troops at Reading, when he acted as Lieutenant of Company I, Fourth Regiment, N. G. P., having arrived home from South America too late to reach Williamsport and go out with his home company.

In 1873 he returned from his position as cashier of an insurance broker's office in New York City to become general manager of the Black Marble operations in the Mosquito Valley, and is still interested with the estate of the late Col. J. D. Potts in this property, having had charge of the prospecting and testing of this marble since 1890.

In 1875 he went to Central America and the East; returning from there he went to South America, traversing the entire continent. He was connected prominently with the expedition in 1878 to build the Maderia and Mamore Railroad (Brazil) in the heart of South America, from San Antonio to Mojimerim, 189 miles. This effort is generally known as the " Collins Expedition," of which the frightful mortality among the employes created consternation in this country. The conducting of the Delaware River tug boats, the " Brazil" and " Juno," from Philadelphia to Brazil, of which he had charge, was considered one of the most dangerous exploits that had been undertaken from this country, particularly so, as the English had tried several times to send some of their tugs to Para and signally failed. These boats were 100, and 85 feet long, drawing 10 and 8 feet of water, respectively. They sailed 3,000 miles straight to sea from Philadelphia, and after being four days without water, breaking down in a West Indian hurricane, and many other dangerous experiences, arrived at Para, Brazil, with every pound of coal in the furnances of the Juno and but one-half ton left in the bunkers of the Brazil. The hazard of this undertaking elicited the remark from a friend : " Well, they couldn't find anybody else to go out in charge of these boats, so they hunted up you."

After some time spent in Europe and South America he settled with his family at Avondale, Chester County, Pa , in 1883, as treasurer of the Baker Lime Company, Limited, which was succeeded in April, 1887, by the Acme Lime Company, Limited, of which he was made chairman. It was while he was thus engaged that a valuable deposit of marble was located by himself and others on the property of the company of which he was chairman, causing, in June, 1893, the industries to be incorporated under the title of the Avondale Marble Company, of which he was made president. This deposit of marble, at present, gives promise of being one of the largest and finest veins in this country, rivaling the famous Vermont and Georgia deposits, and having considerable advantage over them in its location in relation to the large trade centres. He is also a director in other corporations.

Robert Hopewell Hepburn married October 3, 1877, Elizabeth, daughter of Joshua and Gwenllian Thomas Hunt (Joshua Hunt being very prominent in the iron industries of the country,) and granddaughter of David Thomas, famous as the first successful maker of anthracite iron in the United States, and commonly referred to as the "Father of the Iron Interests of Pennsylvania," by whom he has had four children, viz.:

    i. Gwenllian, b. September 19, 1878.
    ii. Andrew Hopewell, b. March 6, 1880.
    iii. George Hunt, b. September 17, 1881.
    iv. Joshua Hunt, b. August 28, 1889.

HEPBURNS OF CLEARFIELD COUNTY, PA.

WILLIAM HEPBURN, born in Donegal, Ireland, about 1779, was of Scotch descent, his ancestors having been driven from Scotland on account of their religious belief. He came to America about 1801 or 1802, and in 1803 made his way up the West Branch of the Susquehanna from Williamsport and settled in the wilderness four miles above what is now Curwensville, and one and a half miles from the river. There he located a tract of land and commenced clearing a farm. The records show that he obtained a warrant (No. 6,031) for 409 acres and 150 perches under date of April 10, 1806, for which he paid $30.39. The patent was issued June 4, 1811. This land laid in what was then Pike (now Penn) Township.

He married, first, about 1814, Miss Mary McCracken, and they had issue:

i. James, b. ———, 1815; d. ———, 1837; unmarried·

ii. Samuel Coleman, b. June 12, 1817. He m. Miss Cynthia Hoover April 17, 1843. Her parents were early settlers on the river a short distance above the town of Clearfield, where she was b. November 20, 1824. They had issue: 1. Joseph, b. May 6, 1845. Is married and lives at Ludington City, Michigan. 2. Erastus W., b. January 13, 1847. Is married and lives in Pennville, Clearfield County, Pa. 3. Mary E., b. May 13, 1849. Married William Moore and resides in Pennville. 4. Levi S., b. November 1, 1851. Married and lives in the borough of Pennville. 5. Samuel T., b. September 20, 1853. Married and lives in Pennville. 6. Martha Elizabeth, b. May 17, 1856. Married Edward Tozier, of Curwensville. 7. Thomas Ross, b. October 18, 1860. Married and lives in Escanaba, Michigan. 8. Lulu, b. April 7, 1867. Single; resides with her parents in Pennville.

iii. John, b. ———, 1821; married Hulda McDonald. They live at Bell's Landing, Clearfield County, and have had issue: 1. William. 2. James.* 3. Mary Ellen. 4. John DeWitt. 5. Hulda M. 6. Martha. 7. Alexander. 8. Charles.

Mrs. Hepburn, the first, having died, William Hepburn married, second, Martha Porter, of Williamsport, and she had one daughter, named Catharine, born in 1823. She married James Thompson, late of Curwensville, and they had three sons and five daughters. The wife of ex-Sheriff Mahaffey, and proprietor of the Windsor Hotel, Clearfield, is one of the daughters.

William Hepburn, progenitor of the family, died in June, 1854, and letters of administration on his estate were taken out by his son, Samuel Coleman, and son-in-law, James Thompson.

---

*In a list of the early members of the bar of Clearfield appears the name of James Hepburn. He was admitted to practice in 1822. What became of him is unknown.

Soon after his settlement in the wilderness near where the Boone family, of Williamsport, had located, Dr. Samuel Coleman came from Williamsport, and purchased a tract of land and set about clearing up a farm. The latter named the Grampian Hills, because they reminded him of his native place in Scotland. Dr. Coleman was a neighbor and friend of William Hepburn; also of James Fleming, a brother-in-law of Hepburn, they having married sisters, the Misses McCracken. Hepburn named his second son Samuel Coleman, after the Doctor, and Fleming named one of his sons after him also.

Dr. Coleman * evidently was greatly pleased at having these two boys named for him, for in his will he devised " unto Samuel Coleman Hepburn and Samuel Coleman Fleming, one-half of two tracts of land (about one thousand acres), one-half of each to be selected by my executors." These lands had been purchased at treasurer's sale by Dr. Coleman in partnership with Arthur Bell. But through lack of attention on the part of the executors in keeping the taxes paid up they were sold again and the two namesakes of Dr. Coleman never realized an acre of what had been willed to them by their generous friend. These lands long since became valuable on account of the pine timber which covered them, and to-day they are worth considerable money.

Samuel Coleman Hepburn is now living with his wife and daughter, at the age of 77, in Pennville,† having retired from

---

* Dr. Samuel Coleman succeeded Dr. William Kent Lathy as the second resident physician of Williamsport about 1804. In 1808 he located in Clearfield County and died in 1819. He left a request in his will to be dressed in his best suit of clothes and buried in one of his fields. As he was the first resident physician of Clearfield County, the Medical Society a few years ago raised a monument over his grave. After remembering his two namesakes he willed all of his estate to Joseph Boone and family. He was unmarried, and never would divulge his paternity.

† The post-office for this borough is called "Grampian," and it (the borough) lies at the terminus of the Tyrone and Clearfield Railroad, twelve miles from Clearfield Town.

active business. His father was a relative of James, William, Samuel and John Hepburn, of Williamsport and Northumberland, but in what degree he cannot tell. They were probably second cousins.

Samuel Coleman Hepburn and his wife, Cynthia, celebrated their golden wedding April 17, 1893. The occasion was a joyous one. The guests were first entertained at the Hepburn residence, where congratulations were extended and old memories revived. At one o'clock the large company assembled in the public hall, where a royal feast was served by friendly hands. The old folks' table was the table of distinction and around it were gathered the following prominent people: Major Luther was accorded the position of toast-master, and Mr. and Mrs. Samuel C. Hepburn were seated at his left. Mr. and Mrs. Nathan Moore, Mr. and Mrs. Thomas Moore, Mr. and Mrs. William Smith, Mr. and Mrs. James Smith, Joseph Davis and wife, Elisha Davis and wife, G. P. Doughman and wife, Levi Speice and wife, J. P. Farwell and wife, Mrs. Catherine Thompson, Mrs. James McIntire, I. B. Norris and wife, M. G. Bloom and wife, Mrs. T. J. Murphy, Mrs. J. Crossley, Mrs. Ross Hoover, Mrs. Sultzbaugh, Mrs. Jonathan Wall, Mrs. Anderson and others whose names we failed to get.

At the other table was a younger set from all parts of the county, G. W. Speice and wife, of Ramey; Milton Speice and wife, of Madera; Dr. Currier and wife, Mr. and Mrs. Quigley, C. L. Frank and wife, Mrs. Jesse Spencer, DuBois; Jack Thompson and wife, Mrs. Will H. Thompson, Curwensville; Chandler Bloom and Miss Haywood, James Leavy, Clearfield; Conductor Hallahan, Insurance Agent Shires and many others.

While all were enjoying the dinner the merriment went the rounds in wave after wave. One party remarked that " the man who could live with one woman for fifty years deserved such a grand time," while the ladies declared that "the woman who could live with a man for fifty years and tolerate him a couple of years before marriage, deserves even more than this."

The after dinner exercises consisted of a solo on the violin by Major Luther, after which Miss Bessie Hepburn recited the following poem:

GRANDMA'S GOLDEN WEDDING.

In olden times, I have been told,
　When husband chose a wife,
One wedding seemed the twain to hold
　Through all their mortal life.

In modern times, if for five years,
　The bond has holden good,
People are coming, it appears,
　To wed again with wood.

If for ten years the twain abide,
　Again the friends come in
To clasp the knot so firmly tied,
　In wedding called the tin.

And yet again, the tried and true,
　When five years more shall pass,
Are wont to celebrate anew
　Their wedding termed the glass.

The Hymen's bond the people learn,
　Grows dear in growing old,
And hence they celebrate in turn
　With China, Silver, Gold.

Thus far they journeyed on their way
　Till fifty years from starting,
And are not you prepared to say
　That they are bent on parting?

A cordial greeting they extend
　To all whose presence bright,
Combines a social joy to lend
　On this, their Golden Night.

Unitedly they pledge you all,
　But not in sparkling wine,
Oh may their loved ones never fall
　Before the mocking shrine.

Then fill the glass for each to-night,
  From nature's crystal tide,
That which has sparkled bright and pure
  Since Grandma became a bride.

How rapidly through all these years
  Life's moments have been fleeting,
Bringing them mingled joys and tears,
  Sad parting and fond greeting.

Eight children from their little band
  Now call them father, mother,
While two are in a distant land,
  Joe and Tom, his brother.

And thus our God in giving joy
  Hath not forgotten chiding,
All earthly bliss has some alloy
  And may not prove abiding.

Yet all along the lights hath shone
  Above the fleeting shadows
Which sometimes settle darkly down
  As fog upon the meadows.

And while the rain may fall to-day,
  The sun will shine to-morrow,
And thus our Father hath always
  Dispelled the clouds of sorrow.

How grateful for the tender care
  Which thus far has been o'er them,
We'll trust our Father to prepare
  The way that lies before them.

In the parlor of the Hepburn residence were displayed many beautiful and golden tokens of love and affection, laid upon the half century marriage altar by relatives and friends. The occasion was one long to be remembered by the principals and their friends.

—◦—

HEPBRON FAMILY, OF MARYLAND.

As early as 1668—possibly earlier—James and Joseph Hepbron emigrated from Scotland and settled on the head-waters of Fishing Creek, in what was afterwards Cecil County, Maryland. It is now known as Lloyd's Creek, and is in Kent County. Joseph never married and died without issue; James married and from him all of the name now living in Kent County claim their descent. Concerning the history of the family, Sewell Hepbron, a descendant, left the following data:

" James * leased or patented a large body of land from the Lord Proprietor of the Province of Maryland, all of which has been sold or alienated from the family, except a small farm of about 200 acres now belonging to Thomas Hepbron. On this farm, which was never sold, is situated the family burying ground in which lie buried all of the Hepbrons that died in this county previous to the year 1829, and some who have died since.

" The name, as I find from old papers and parchments, has been variously spelled Hepbron, Hepbourn, Hepron and Hepburn, which last mode, I have no doubt, is the correct way of spelling it. I have seen the old parchment for the first grant of land to James Hepbron, as the name was then spelled, from Lord Baltimore. It was burned, with many other old and quaint relics, with the old mansion, about the year 1844.

" The first generation or two in this country (as I suppose they were in Scotland), were Catholics; but I find (History of Old Kent, p. 356), that on April 2, 1716, (Records of Shrewsbury Parish), Thomas Hepbourn was elected one of the vestrymen, and again on April 6, 1724. I find that Sewell Hepbron was register, and his son, Sewell S. Hepbron, rector of I. U. Parish.

---

* On page 530, Vol. 1, of Sabines Loyalists of the Revolution, occurs this reference: " Hepburn, James, of North Carolina. He was attached to a corps of Loyalists as secretary, and in 1776 was taken prisoner and confined. He was in New York in 1782, and a notary public." Possibly he was a descendant of James Hepbron, of Maryland.

"Much that I have written I have gathered from my old uncle, Thomas Hepbron. He used to delight me much when a boy by exhibiting to us boys the old family jewels that had descended to him as the oldest male heir. Among them were many quaint old rings, knee and shoe buckles, bracelets, etc., of massive gold set with brilliants, which were heirlooms of the family, and had regularly descended from his Scottish ancestors.

"I have been with him to the family grave-yard where he has pointed out the spot where old James Hepbron lies buried, and over whose grave is now growing a large walnut tree. In searching the records of this county you will find the name but rarely mentioned. The Hepbrons were a quiet, honest and unobtrusive race. Not one of them, up to this time (1875), that I have ever heard of, has ever held or asked for an office."

Another descendant, W. Hepbron, writes under date of April 11, 1891, to a member of the Williamsport family, from whose letter the following extracts are taken:

"I have always understood from the old heads of our family that we are of Scottish descent, and that we were mixed up in some way with the Earls of Bothwell; also that the name of Hepburn has its origin in two rivers of Scotland.

"The original papers of the land grant from Lord Baltimore to Thomas Hepbron were burned years ago with the old mansion house. * * * We lost a Samuel Hepbron years ago, I am told. He left home on horseback to go to Philadelphia to buy goods and no account has been heard of him since, though my father, James Hepbron, used every means possible to find what became of him. My father, I am told, got the horse he rode.

"My uncle Sewell, now dead, took a great interest in hunting up the records of the family, and for the history we now have we are indebted to his efforts. I am sure that I have heard him say that there was a branch of the family at Williamsport, Pa., and that the Hepburns were the builders of the place. * * * It is a singular fact that the old names have been kept in the family. We have two Louis Hepbrons—their names were never spelled Lewis, but Louis."

The most striking of the names that have been preserved on the female side of the house are Janet, and on the male side Samuel, James and John. Janet has been handed down from Patrick Hepburn, the first Earl of Bothwell (1488–1508), who married Lady *Janet* Douglas, who became the mother of three sons and three daughters, one of whom was named Janet, and the name has been handed down to the present time. From this Earl it is believed that all the early Hepburns in America were descended.

—◦—

THE CONNECTICUT BRANCH.

Three brothers named Hepburn settled in Connecticut at an early period in the history of New England. Mrs. Mary A. (Hepburn) Smith, of Milford, Connecticut, and a descendant, writes that their names were Patrick, James and John. One of the brothers, it seems, had become involved in some rebellion or conspiracy, and fled from Scotland about 1680. It is probable that it was what is known in history as the Oates Rebellion. In a short time his two brothers came, to be with him, and make a home here. Mrs. Smith says:

"They must have been of some importance, as they brought a copy of their coat of arms, a canteen or drinking cup (as they called it), which was a gourd shell mounted in silver and inscribed on the top: 'Patrick Hepburn, Abbey-millom, 1640.' Also silver shoe and knee buckles. I have in my possession a little trunk which, tradition asserts, was brought by them also.

" My great-grandfather, Peter Hepburn, was a sea captain, and having a cargo for Glasgow, took the papers in his possession with the intention of proving his identity and claiming property to which he and his relatives were entitled. The story handed down to us was this: After discharging his cargo he took the papers and went twelve miles up the Clyde, visited the church, had a long conversation with the sexton, who said his father was sexton before him and he had often heard him tell of the brothers leaving home, etc. Great-grandfather made an appointment to go the next day and attend to the business of establishing his claim. He then returned to Glasgow and remained at the inn near the wharf over night. While eating his breakfast next morning the inn-keeper came in with a newspaper in his hand saying: ' Great news, great news this morning!' 'What news?' 'Why, the King has declared the colonies in rebellion, and I hope he will hang every mother's son of them!'

" Great-grandfather continued his breakfast, but, as he often said in relating it, kept up a deil of a thinking as to what he had better do if the news were true, finally saying to himself, ' Peter Hepburn, you have a wife and children across this big pond; which are of more importance, family history, lands, etc., or your duty to them?' Turning to the inn-keeper he said: ' There is one thing he will have to do before he hangs them.' 'What is that?' 'He will have to catch them first.'

" By that time he had made up his mind to put his ship in ballast and cut for home, where he arrived in safety, trusting to the future for the establishing of claims.

" The place twelve miles from Glasglow was no doubt Bothwell Castle and manse where he was to examine the records. My theory is that we descended from George, son of the second Earl of Bothwell, and they lived in Humbick; my father said a place that sounds 'Ambic.'

"In the life of Sir John Hepburn, by James Grant, there is a description of that home, and also the giving to Isabella, his sister, by George, of the Abbeymill property.

"There is not much doubt as to the brothers who came here in 1680 being Catholics, as you will remember there is nothing said of Protestantism in Scotland until Queen Mary's and John Knox's time, which was in the latter part of the third Earl of Bothwell and the commencement of the fourth Earl's [James Hepburn] time. It is said he became a Protestant, and that was one of the reasons why Mary's half-brother, Murray, was so bitter against him. Although he is defamed in history, I have always had great sympathy for him, and judge him by the time he lived in.

"The immediate ancestors of the Pennsylvania branch probably fled to the north of Ireland and there embraced the Protestant faith. I have visited among some of the Maryland Hepbrons. I do not think any of them are Romanists at this time. * * * The Wilkes-Barre Hepburns are of the Connecticut branch. I have never heard from what the family took its name. I do not think it has ever been considered a clan, but a family, great and powerful, as far back as 1200. They were not Border Highlanders, but educated people for the times."

Mrs. Smith, who spent many years of her married life in New York, has, since the death of her husband, occupied the ancestral home at Milford, Connecticut, during the summer months, and the winter season in Washington City. For several years she has been engaged in collecting the genealogy and history of her branch of the family, with the view of publishing it for the benefit of the numerous descendants of Patrick, James and John Hepburn.

HON. W. P. HEPBURN, OF IOWA.

James Hepburn, a native of Scotland, came to this country during the latter part of the last century and settled in

New York City.   He married Miss Frances Lynch, a lady
of German descent.   They had issue :

i. Samuel.
ii. Frances.
iii. James S., b. January 1, 1800.
iv. Frederick.
v. Ellen.

James S., the third child, was a cadet at the United States
Military Academy, West Point, July 31, 1814, to July 1,
1819, when he was graduated and appointed Second Lieutenant, Corps of Artillery; transferred to the Fourth Artillery June 1, 1821; transferred to the Second Artillery August 16, 1821, and resigned October 1, 1824.   After leaving
the service he was a physician at New Orleans, La., where
he died May 2, 1833, aged 33 years, 4 months and 1 day.

He married Miss Ann F., daughter of Dr. Hanson Cat-
lett, surgeon in the United States Army, at Pittsburg, Pa.
They had seven children, of whom but the following survive :

i. William Peters Hepburn, b. November 4, 1833, at
     Wellsville, Columbiana County, Ohio.
ii. Fannie M.

William Peters, the son, was taken to Iowa (then a territory) in April, 1841.   He was educated in the schools of
the territory and in a printing office.   Studied law and was
admitted to practice law in 1854; served in the Second Iowa
Cavalry as Captain, Major and Lieutenant Colonel during
the war of the Rebellion.   He was a delegate from Iowa to
the Republican National Convention of 1860 and 1888; was
a Presidential Elector-at-Large for the state of Iowa in 1876
and 1888.   Colonel Hepburn was elected to the Forty-
seventh, Forty-eighth and Forty-ninth Congresses and re-
elected to the Fifty-third Congress as a Republican, receiving 20,219 votes over Thomas H. Maxwell, Democrat, who
received 15,968; Scott, Populist, who received 3,687 votes,

and Dobbs, Prohibitionist, who received 834 votes, and re-elected to the Fifty-fourth Congress by a large plurality. Colonel Hepburn's place of residence is Clarinda, Page County, Iowa.

ANCESTRY AND HISTORY OF A. B. HEPBURN.

Hon. A. B. Hepburn, president of the Third National Bank, New York, and Comptroller of the Currency during the last year of President Harrison's administration, is a descendant of Peter Hepburn, a native of Scotland, and who died in Stratford, Connecticut, in 1742. His wife was Sarah Hubbell, of Newtown, Connecticut, and after the death of her husband she returned there to live with her three younger children. Their children, all born in Stratford, were:

  i. Joseph, b. October 11, 1729.
 ii. Peter, b. April 24, 1732.
iii. Sarah, b. July 24, 1736.
 iv. George, b. May 12, 1739.

Joseph, their eldest son, married Eunice Burton, of Stratford, daughter of Judson Burton and Eunice Lewis. She was born in 1732, and admitted to full membership and communion in the Congregational Church, of Stratford, at the age of ten years. Joseph, first, and Eunice were married November 4, 1751, and had issue, all born in Statford:

   i. Joseph, second, b. July 28, 175-.
  ii. Silas, b. February ——, 1756.
 iii. Lewis, b. October ——, 1763.
  iv. Patrick, b. October ——, 1766.
   v. George, b. September ——, 1768.
  vi. Eunice, b. ——— ———, ——; m. Miles Hotchkiss.
 vii. Sarah, b.——— ———, ——; never married.
viii. Ana, b.——— ———, ——.

Joseph, second, born July 28, 1752, married Hannah Lobdell, and they settled in Hotchkisstown, Connecticut, now Westville, on the outskirts of New Haven, where they lived for some years. They had issue:

i. Patrick, b. February 1, 1778 ; m. June 25, 1808, Sallie Hitchcock.
ii. Almena, b. May 9, 1779.
iii. Roderick, b. February 3, 1780 ; m. Amarilla Hitchcock.
iv. Betsy, b. December 19, 1780.
v. Vileroy, b. August 7, 1783.
vi. Martha, b. February 2, 1786.
vii. Marhetta, b. July, ——, 1787.
viii. Suderick, b. May 23, 1789.
ix. Hannah, b. October 21, 1792.
x. Joseph, b. October 30, 1794.
xi. Pliny, b. December 5, 1796.
xii. Zina E., b. October 13, 1798, in Middlebury, Vermont.

Zina E. Hepburn, born October 13, 1798 ; died September 14, 1874. He married Beulah Gray, who was born March 16, 1807, in St. Lawrence County, N. Y., and is still living. They had issue, all born at Colton, St. Lawrence County, N. Y., excepting the eldest, who was born at Waddington, same County :

i. Chloe I., b. June 16, 1830; d. November 17, 1866.
ii. George W., b. July 3, 1832.
iii. Coedelia A., b. July 28, 1834.
iv. Edwin B., b. April 30, 1837.
v. Hawley S., b. March 2, 1840.
vi. Alonzo Barton, b. July 24, 1846.
vii. Myron H., b. November 25, 1849.

ALONZO BARTON HEPBURN,[5] (Zina,[4] Joseph,[3] Joseph,[2] Peter,[1]) born in Colton, New York, July 24, 1846, traces his lineage (as indicated above) back to Peter Hepburn. Just when his great-great-grandfather came to this country is unknown (probably about 1700), but he died in Stratford, Connecticut, in 1742.

The life and public services of Mr. A. B. Hepburn, as sketched in *The Banking Law Journal* (Vol. VIII., pp. 49–50), are as follows :

Mr. Hepburn fitted for college at St. Lawrence Academy,

Potsdam, N. Y., and Falley Seminary, Fulton, N. Y., and entered the Middlebury College, Marlborough, Vt., in the class of 1871, which institution he left in his Sophomore year, owing to sickness. He afterwards became Professor of Mathematics in St. Lawrence Academy, and was principal of the Ogdensburg Educational Institute in the year 1870. He was soon after admitted to the bar and commmenced the practice of law at Colton.

His first public office was that of school commissioner of the second district of St. Lawrence County, which position he held for three years and a half, resigning to take his seat in the New York Assembly the first of January, 1875. He represented his district in the Legislature for five successive years, during which period he served on the committee on Railroads, Insurance, Judiciary, Ways and Means, and other important committees, devoting his attention to commercial and financial interests, canals, railroads and insurance. As chairman of the Insurance Committee he introduced, among other important measures, and secured the passage of the law making life-insurance policies non-forfeitable after the payment of three annual premiums, and requiring the companies upon application to issue paid-up insurance to an amount which the surrender value of the policy would purchase at regular rates. He was chairman of the Railroad Investigation Committee, raised at the instance of the Chamber of Commerce of the city of New York, Board of Trade, Transportation and other commercial bodies of the state; took over 6,000 pages of testimony, and reported to the Legislature several important measures which became laws; among them an act creating the present Railroad Commission, an act regulating the use of proxies, and an act defining and regulating annual reports, compelling a continuous balance sheet. Prior to this act, the railroad reports had been a source of confusion rather than of information to an investigator.

In April, 1880, he was appointed by Governor Cornell, superintendent of the banking department of the state of New York, a position which he held something over three years and until succeeded by Willis S. Paine, under Governor Cleveland's administration.

In 1883 he was appointed receiver, and wound up the

affairs of the Continental Life Insurance Company of the city of New York.

In June, 1889, he was appointed National Bank Examiner for the cities of New York and Brooklyn, by Comptroller Lacey and the late Secretary Windom, from which position he was promoted by President Harrison July 27, 1892, to be Comptroller of the Currency.

In the early part of the month of January, 1890, a party of schemers purchased the control of the Sixth National Bank, one of our strongest up-town banks, paying a large premium per share for it. The same parties in interest, or their friends, had previously bought a controlling interest in the Lenox Hill Bank and the Equitable Bank. The checks of the Lenox Hill Bank were redeemed through the Sixth National Bank at the clearing house; those of the Equitable were made through the Western National Bank. To reimburse the ring for the payment of so large a sum for the controlling interest of the Sixth National Bank, immediately upon having elected themselves as directors, they commenced to make loans to themselves on various questionable securities, and also to sell the good assets of the Sixth National. The cashier, Mr. Colston, connected with the bank for more than a quarter of a century, becoming alarmed at the questionable transfers, notified the clearing house, and at this juncture, Mr. Hepburn, who was then National Bank Examiner, was called in. By his prompt action in obtaining partial restitution from these bank wreckers, a large amount of money was saved for the bank, and the bank was allowed to resume business as soon as the complications arising from the abstraction of its securities had been adjusted. The principal conspirators were sent to state's prison. Mr. Hepburn's previous connection with the banking department of this state, and his broad knowledge of the affairs of the various banks, and their clearing-house agents at that time, served to doubly justify the wisdom of his appointment as National Bank Examiner for the city of New York. His administration of this office was characteristic of the man, and it is conceded by all who know, that his examinations were the most thorough ever made by any examiner in New York City.

About the time of his retirement from the position of

Comptroller of the Currency, United States Treasury, Mr. Hepburn was chosen president of the Third National Bank, Nassau Street, New York City, the duties of which he is now performing. That it is one of the great financial institutions of New York may be inferred from the fact that it has a capital of one million dollars. The statement for July 18, 1894, shows that its loans and discounts were $7,522,357.06, and the deposits were $12,283,271.48. The amount of business covered reached the enormous total of $13,775,034.38.

" The financial centres," remarks *The Banking Law Journal*, " which are more or less affected by good banking in New York, are to be congratulated upon having [had] one so thorough and efficient in control of the very important bureau at Washington." And, with equal propriety, it may be added, they are to be congratulated on having him in their midst now as the head of one of the great banking houses of the city. Continuing, the same authority says : " Mr. Hepburn is a man of broad mind and great executive ability, and is eminently qualified in every respect to fill the position."

Mr. Hepburn married, first, Harriet A. Fisher, of St. Alban's, Vermont, December 10, 1873. She died December 28, 1881, leaving issue :

   i. Harold Barton, b. April 5, 1876; d. March 27, 1892.
   ii. Charles Fisher, b. July 14, 1878. Now in Worcester (Massachusetts) Academy, fitting for college.

Having remained a widower over six years, Mr. Hepburn married, second, Emily L. Eaton, of Montpelier, Vermont, July 14, 1887, and they have one daughter, born August 28, 1890.

THE END.

INDEX.

www.ingramcontent.com/pod-product-compliance
Lightning Source LLC
Chambersburg PA
CBHW070913270326
41927CB00011B/2553